DISCARD

Cyber *Lies*

When Finding the Truth Matters

John Paul Lucich

FOREWORD BY DR. LUANN LINQUIST

STARPATH
BOOKS

BAS PS

The cases referred to in this book are real, but all identifying information has been changed to ensure the confidentiality of those involved.

Published by: StarPath Books, LLC
759 Bloomfield Avenue, # 328
West Caldwell, New Jersey 07006
(888) 674-4872

ISBN-13: 978-0-9774894-0-4   ISBN-10: 0-9774894-0-X
Library of Congress Control Number: 2005909703

Front Cover: Roger Janik, ServerSideDesign.com   Cover Model: Vikki Ziegler
Book Design: Janice Marie Phelps
PRINTED IN THE UNITED STATES OF AMERICA

Limits of Liability and Disclaimer of Warranty

Nothing contained in this book is to be considered as the rendering of advice for any specific case, and readers are respon-sible for obtaining such advice from their own expert or legal counsel. This book is intended for educational and informational purposes only.

The author and publisher of this book have used their best efforts in preparing the book and the instructions contained in it. These efforts include the development, research, and or testing of the instructions and or programs to determine their effectiveness. The author and publisher make no warranty of any kind, expressed or implied, with regard to these instructions, and or programs referenced in this book and expect that readers will comply with all laws that affect their jurisdiction.

The author and publisher shall not be liable in the event of inci-dental or consequential damages in connection with, or arising out of, the furnishing, performance, or use of the instructions, programs and/or claims of productivity gains.

35.00   1344909   12/6/06

To my wife and children, who gave up their time with me and supported my efforts that I might finish this book.

To my clients and others whose painful experiences are the foundation of this book and whose stories have touched my life.

Trademark Acknowledgments

In following standard book style, the trademark symbol is placed at the first mention of a trademark name. Trademark names are also listed below. The following list of companies, or the mention of any company anywhere in *Cyber Lies,* does *not* imply endorsement. In fact, no endorsements have been made.

Accurate Outlook Express Mail Expert™ is a trademark of Accurate Solution

AOL™ is a trademark of America Online™, Inc.

Book-of-the-Month Club® is a registered trademark of BookSpan

Cell Seizure™ is a trademark of Paraben Corporation

DBXanalyzer™ is a trademark of DI Management Services Pty Ltd

FTK™ is a trademark of Access Data Corporation

Google™ is a trademark of Google, Inc.

Linux® is a registered trademark of Linus Torvalds

MailNavigator™ is a trademark of GEO Ltd.

Microsoft™, MSN™, Outlook Express™, Windows™, Windows Explorer™ and Windows Internet Explorer™ are trademarks of Microsoft Corporation

Mozilla Firefox® is a registered trademark of the Mozilla Corp.

Palm® Treo™ is a registered trademark of Palm®, Inc.

PDA Seizure™ is a trademark of Paraben Corporation

Post-it® is a registered trademark of 3M

Quickbooks™ is a trademark of Intuit, Inc.

Quicktime™ is a trademark of Apple, Inc.

Registry Viewer™ is a trademark of Access Data Corporation

Yahoo!® is a registered trademark of Yahoo!, Inc.

Table of Contents

Foreword

Dr. Luann Linquist, MFT, MCC

Men and women cheat on their spouses at an alarming rate. Research shows that between 52 and 73 percent of people are in a relationship with a cheater. How do you find out if you are one of them? Do you know or suspect you are, but can't prove it? *Cyber Lies,* by John Lucich, is your expert guide to get access to hidden and, until now, out-of-reach technical information that reveals what you need to know.

Through more than twenty years of counseling victims of affairs, and as the author of *SECRET LOVERS . . . How to Cope,* I discovered the major driver of the increase in cheating/affairs is the ease that technology offers. It provides not only temptation — which has always been there in many forms — but also instant gratification: "Just take a peek; click here; someone to talk to; someone is here waiting for you now." There also is the constant barrage of spam that simply encourages you to "try it, you'll like it." It's very enticing and seductive.

I have helped hundreds of people through the pain and suffering caused by lies and secrets. Many times, after much resistance and even more lies to keep their secrets, the cheater is relieved when their deceit is finally out in the open. This is a vulnerable time for a relationship because emotions are very high, swinging between guilt, anger, hurt, and fear of loss.

But there is hope. An affair does not have to ruin a good relationship. You can and will get through this. Couples I've worked with are a testament to the human ability to heal the hurts, stay together, and even improve their relationships.

The first step is to find the truth. This is why reading *Cyber Lies* is so important: Mr. Lucich helps you **find the truth**. You become informed sooner, rather than later. Your knowledge helps eliminate the days, months, and years of the drama cycle (Suspicion-Hurt-Deception) that weigh heavily on any relationship.

Yes, secret, private, supposedly "no-big-deal" time spent in chat rooms, Instant-Messaging (IM), frequent e-mails, quickie cell calls, and visits to cheating and dating Internet websites are as serious a threat to your relationship as a face-to-face, belly-to-belly affair.

Whether it is just a fling, an ongoing affair, sexual addiction, or lack of moral compass, Lucich — with easy-to-use, no-nonsense tools and straightforward talk — gives you a way to take charge. No longer will you be on the receiving end of a cheater's poor choices.

I am highly impressed with *Cyber Lies.* John Lucich is a law enforcement veteran, college professor, and internationally recognized computer forensic expert. He knows the basis of the technology behind computers and cell phones, which offer a fertile environment for spouses who are inclined to cheat.

If you are the innocent spouse/partner, *Cyber Lies* arms you with the information you need to gain a better understanding of technology, the methods to protect yourself, and the how-tos of accessing the technological devices to obtain the data to make crucial, important, and difficult decisions.

Cyber Lies isn't a training manual for learning how to be a computer forensic expert, nor is it a handbook for repairing your marriage. Mr. Lucich is your guide to understanding how you can take advantage of computer technology and cell phones to end the cheat-by-deceit drama.

Even if you are not technically advanced, all you need is determination to help yourself and your lawyers in discovering what has been deleted from computer files or the name and address connected to the cell phone number you found written on a Post-it® note. *Cyber Lies* even helps you solve the mystery of keystrokes from the late-night IM chat going on downstairs when your spouse told you, "We were just working late."

Many faithful spouses cannot afford to hire a computer forensic expert. And, sometimes there simply isn't time to find one. John Lucich brings this forensic expertise to you in *Cyber Lies*. He wrote this book to help you get started NOW by accessing, imaging, and reviewing computer information that can help you learn the reality of your situation.

You can almost hear Lucich's confident voice and discerning advice when *Cyber Lies* is open to "Steps For Imaging a Hard Drive," and your monitor is displaying the hidden, and until-now-secret "lovey-dovey" e-mails from "single_guy@anynet.net" to "ready_now@bored.com."

Readers' Tips:

To assist the reader in following the directions in *Cyber Lies* the following type styles are used throughout the book:

- Computer keys are indicated in **boldface** type and ALL CAPS, with the exception of the "Page Up" key which is noted as follows: **PgUp.**

- Computer commands, screens, icons, menu items, windows and options are listed in **boldface** type with the inital letter capped.

- File names, passwords, account names, file folders, login names, and user names are indicated in plain font with ALL CAPS.

- Long file paths are in standard text font.

- Clicking the mouse buttons – If the directions do not indicate clicking the *left* or *right* button on the mouse, click the left button.

Cyber Lies was written specifically for the Windows™ operating system. However, when referencing the technical how-to section of this book, you may notice small nuances between Windows XP Professional™ and Windows 2000 Professional™. In addition, there may be even greater differences in the earlier Windows operating systems such as Windows95™, Windows98™ and the Windows Millennium Edition™. All of these operating systems will be supported by either this book or the *Cyber Lies* website. So, if you are using an older operating system and do not see what the book is describing, then simply reference the website at www.cyberlies.com/support. If you do not find the information you need, please send an email to support@cyberlies.com.

Welcome to My World

Starting Off with the Right Tools

Cyber Lies is an indispensable tool for readers interested in locating, retrieving, reviewing, and analyzing information stored on technological devices – in other words, computer forensics and data recovery. By reading *Cyber Lies,* you will learn the basic steps that will enable you to quickly gain access to crucial information located on cell phones and computers. For readers facing the stresses and complications of going through a divorce, *Cyber Lies* will show you how to obtain the data you need to discover and document if your spouse is cheating on you or if they are involved in inappropriate online activities.

Knowledge Is Power

In addition to accessing crucial data, through *Cyber Lies,* readers also will acquire knowledge about how to *recover* deleted data from hard drives and preserve the resulting potential evidence by imaging the hard drive. Imaging a hard drive means to make an exact duplicate of the entire hard drive and then store that data in evidence files for later review. If you later need to hire a computer forensic expert, you can, thus, provide them with the image files for their examination and analysis.

It is important for readers to understand that they are not computer forensic experts, nor are they trying to be. Their efforts should be focused on gaining access to crucial data for analysis. In addition, this book provides a reader with several options on how to proceed based on their own circumstances. In some cases, this may be through the use of forensic tools and methodologies, while in other cases it may just involve the copying of certain data for analysis. In these types of cases, a reader may inadvertently change the dates and times of files as they access the computer to copy data.

Typically, changing file dates and times may not be an issue in some cases. For example, an INBOX.DBX file contains messages received for Microsoft Outlook Express™. As you may know, Microsoft Outlook Express is an e-mail program that enables a person to send and receive e-mail messages. The date and time of the INBOX.DBX file has absolutely no relevance to the dates and times of the messages contained in that file. So, when you access the INBOX.DBX file, the *file last accessed* date and time changes, but the dates and times of the internal messages remain unmodified. What counts on these occasions are the messages contained in the INBOX.DBX file, so don't worry if you do not have a very technical background.

In my experience, most of the time the information important to spouses is easily accessible using the methodologies described in this book and often does not require the services of a computer forensic expert. One exception would be when the results of the forensic acquisition or data are challenged in a court of law. Recovered e-mail messages, instant-messaging logs, and other types of data documenting intimate relationships or online activity are the most crucial in divorce cases; and *Cyber Lies* will examine accessing and recovering such data. Remember, I wrote this book for *you*. No one, including your attorney or the judge, expects you to be a computer forensic expert. The only trait they expect from you is honesty.

Cyber Lies will teach you how to review a variety of technological devices that might be used by your spouse. These may include cell phones and computers. Many readers will want to use the information they have gleaned by reading *Cyber Lies,* but the book is not intended to replace the use of a computer forensic expert. If you know at the start that you are going to hire an expert, then read this book all the way through, but remember – *Do not touch the computer!* After reading *Cyber Lies,* you will have a useful understanding of computer forensics and be better able to communicate with the expert, thus giving them the information they need to do the best job for you.

A note for readers who do not *intend to hire a computer forensic expert: Cyber Lies* is not intended to be a training manual to be used for readers wishing to become computer forensic experts. I realize, however, that not everyone can afford to hire a computer forensic expert. Or, there may be emergent instances when you do not have the time to go through the process of hiring an expert, but you do need to take immediate action. This is where *Cyber Lies* can be extremely helpful to you.

What Cyber Lies Cannot Do for You

It is important to me that you are successful in your endeavors to recover computer data. If, however, you were looking for a book to help you save your relationship, *Cyber Lies* is not the book. A cursory browse through bookstore shelves will enable you to become familiar with hundreds of books written by medical doctors, Ph.D.s, and "love experts" that can point you in the right direction. Over the years, I have been hired by many lawyers and their clients in numerous divorce cases, and I have had access to the most intimate details of their experiences. During those times, I have tried to be as supportive to clients as I could, so I know what you are going through. I know what and how you are feeling, I know the level of frustration that you will reach, and I also know how important it is to you to find solutions. That is why I wrote *Cyber Lies.* To help you. So please read the *entire* book. Don't get tempted to jump past certain chapters because you have browsed through the Table of Contents thinking the content of those chapters may not be relevant to your needs and you are eager to get started reviewing data immediately. There is important information in every one of the chapters – details that you need to know before starting to work on any computer or cell phone. Give yourself the time you need to absorb and comprehend the material, and you will be successful.

Rush through this book, and you increase the potential to misunderstand the instructions or even destroy the data you are attempting to recover. It is also important to read the chapters in the order they appear. I have written the book in building-block fashion, so each chapter builds on the next, and each prior chapter supports the current chapter.

Helping Your Lawyer to Help You

Before I begin talking about computer forensics and accessing data stored on a variety of technological devices, I want to touch briefly on a subject that is going to be absolutely crucial to obtaining the most successful outcome possible in a potential divorce proceeding. It is the one part on which you should expend an enormous amount of effort and pay close attention to. If you don't, all of your work retrieving data will be meaningless and you will be left miserable and blaming everyone except your cheating spouse.

Some people respond to their frustration and lack of motivation by blaming their lawyer. Keep in mind that a good lawyer can try their utmost to get you the best possible settlement, but they can't guarantee it. The outcome of your case will depend on you, your lawyer, your spouse, your spouse's lawyer, the judge, the facts of the case, the evidence you present, and much more. If you have an uncooperative spouse or your spouse's attorney is more disruptive rather that constructive, all of this can adversely affect your case. In the end, it was your spouse who brought you to this point in your life. Being mindful of this and keeping your lawyer up to date on all your activities as they relate to your divorce proceedings will help you immensely. Don't do anything without your lawyer's approval no matter how wrong you feel your lawyer may be. Divorce proceedings can put many of us through an emotional and stressful time that we may not be able to fully handle and react to in an appropriate way. Since your divorce lawyer is not involved emotionally, they're best able to see things more clearly and help direct you through the fog of bitterness. Listen to them and let them guide you. Isn't that what you hired them for?

The most important aspect of your divorce proceedings will be choosing a lawyer to represent you. So you must make every effort to ensure that it is the most informed decision possible. While most people going through a divorce would love to choose the attorney for the *opposing* spouse, this is not going to happen. It would also be great if you got to choose the judge, but this is not possible either. So in the one aspect of your divorce where you actually get to make a choice – the person who will represent your interests – make sure you choose wisely.

When selecting a lawyer, remember that they – like other professionals – have different skill sets, different personalities, and different levels of determination and patience. It is important that you make an informed decision when hiring a divorce lawyer. Speaking with the attorney and checking references should help provide you with enough information to be confident in making a decision. In my experience, some of the best traits that I have seen in lawyers are a sense of determination, compassion, and obligation to their clients. There are a lot of highly qualified and truly gifted attorneys and I hope you find one to represent you. That being said, let's get back to the topic of this book.

Preparing Yourself for Action

Welcome to my world. It can be a bizarre place at times, but it is never boring. One of the reasons for this is that in the realm of cheating spouses, the bar for inappropriate behavior has reached a new low. Therefore, before you enter my world, you must understand the philosophy that I adhere to: *Trust no one and suspect everyone.* I really don't suggest you should live your life by this maxim, but I do want you to be successful in your endeavors with regard to identifying, locating, and recovering the information that you are seeking. Therefore, while you pursue these activities, you must adhere to the philosophy that is necessary in the world of computer forensics.

Before you take the first step, I would like to give you a warning and some advice. Have you ever heard the phrase, *Be careful what you wish for?* In your quest for the realities of your situation, you are asking me to show you how to access information regarding your spouse or partner. In *Cyber Lies,* I will tell you where and how to find this data. However, what you find during your investigation may not be what you are ready to see – so prepare yourself. Just like Neo was asked to choose the blue pill or red pill in *The Matrix,* you now have that same choice. Choose the blue pill by placing this book back on the shelf and walking away, or choose the red pill by continuing to read this book. Be forewarned that just like Neo, there is no turning back, and you may soon have something unsettling and unfamiliar stuck in the back of your head that you can't remove or ignore. That something may be information documenting your spouse's online or extramarital activities.

Okay, so you chose the red pill. Great choice.

I'm sure that the next question you have is, *What will I need to do to prepare myself emotionally?* The level of emotional preparation that you will need is proportionate to the level of concern you currently have regarding your spouse's activities. If you are merely concerned about their recent activities, but cannot pinpoint any event where you know your spouse lied or misled you, then you may not find anything in your search for the truth. However, if you have strong suspicions about specific actions, then fasten your seatbelt because you may find yourself on a wild ride needing to make rapid, life-changing decisions. Unfortunately, I see more of the latter in my business, and it has led to both heartbreak and despair. Almost every time one of my clients has a strong suspicion that their spouse is involved in an affair or addicted to some type of online perversion, I routinely find the evidence to support those suspicions, and frequently I find a lot of it.

Today's Reality Check

Our society has been gradually moving toward an attitude of self-grati-fication – a kind of attitude that says, *Me first!* This is probably one of the major reasons that relationships between spouses fail. People say the old days are gone forever. You may remember the days when people stuck together through trying times and worked problems out for the benefit of the children. Not today. The new relationship model is: *Do what makes me feel good right now.* Working things out is too hard for too many people, and it does not satisfy their immediate need for pleasure. We have become a selfish society, and those of us who refuse to follow the status quo are often destined for disappointment. This is true unless you know how to find out if your spouse is just as committed to the relationship as you are. This is important knowledge to have, as it is often the things that we don't know that can hurt us the most.

Today there are plenty of things that can distract from the relationship we have with our spouse or life partner and, unfortunately, we may find that the person is not the same person we thought they were. Most people enter a relationship with the greatest of intentions, and then life comes in and beats the living hell out of both of them. Is that fair? No, but life isn't always fair. Some people enter relationships as a convenience. It's good enough for them until the next opportunity comes along. Is that fair? No, it's not; and it can often lead to devastation and financial burdens, not to mention heartache and agony for the other spouse.

Life is life, but sometimes it's also what we make of it. It can be as strong as we are and it can be as weak as we are. No matter what life gives us, however, we are individually and solely responsible for the decisions that we make, and we must understand that those decisions can and will often have repercussions that not only affect us but those around us. It is truly unfortunate when one spouse makes decisions that dramatically and drastically affect the other. If you are on the receiving end of your spouse's poor choices, it is important for you to understand that it is not *your* fault. You are not to blame for your spouse's cheating. I have seen too many people spending emotional energy analyzing themselves on why their spouses cheated. Remember, it's *them*, not you. I don't need a degree in psychology to tell you that it's their weakness, not yours; it is in no way a reflection on your ability to maintain a good relationship. This is the very premise of why I wrote *Cyber Lies: To arm you with the information you need to gain a better understanding of technology, to provide you with the methods to protect yourself, and to access technological devices to obtain the data to make crucial decisions.* This book is designed to be part of your support system. I wrote this book for the person who is committed to their relationship, even though their spouse may not be. *Cyber Lies* will help you identify information that can assist you in making decisions that will eventually help you to protect yourself. I cannot make any decision for you, nobody can. What I can do is show you how to uncover information that will help provide a direction for you. In the event that your spouse has decided to leave you for another, this book will show you how to maintain and protect your privacy, while uncovering information and facts that may assist you as you proceed through a potential legal process.

Spouses who have been through a rough relationship sometimes just want the truth. They not only need it, but they deserve it. It's not always about the legal process, it's not always about the law, and it's not always about getting even. A lawyer will tell you that your divorce case is not about your spouse cheating on you. Rather, the goal should be dissolving the marriage, dividing the assets, and in a growing number of cases − child custody. I have, however, worked too many cases to know that for the faithful spouse, the truth is what's important. They have been told by their spouse that they are "crazy," that they are "paranoid," and that they are *wrong* about their suspicions. Remember: *Cheaters lie.* Cheating spouses will often tell their spouse that they love them and frequently try to place the blame for their suspicions back on them. A wife once asked me, "Am I crazy?"

I replied, "Here, look at these nude pictures of your husband that he was sending out via e-mail to other women. No, you're not crazy! He is."

In my seventeen years as a law enforcement officer, my last eight and half years were spent with the New Jersey Attorney General's Office, State Organized Crime and Racketeering Bureau seizing computers from a variety of criminals. These computers were subsequently analyzed to prove criminal offenses. In addition, I spent another ten years in the corporate sector analyzing computers for trade secret violations, network intrusions, sexual harassment, discrimination, and divorce cases. You could say that I have seen it all and that nothing surprises me anymore: criminal activity and sexual perversion taken to extremes; good people drawn into horrible situations because they were drawn away by their lusts; people who have come close to losing it all − family and fortunes.

Winning Sometimes Means Losing

How much do you think a fling with a coworker would cost? Try over $300,000.00 in legal bills, *and* the defendant won the case. Winning is such a subjective word when you end up risking everything that is important to you. And, it is not just men who are cheating. Women also fall victim to their desires and have just as much – if not more – to lose. In one case, for example, a wife was having an affair with the babysitter. When her friend went back to college, the relationship did not end. E-mail messages and instant-messaging all documented their feelings toward each other, while other communications documented her promiscuity.

In another case, a wife suspected that her husband was having an affair with an old college friend. He swore that they were just friends; that is, until I found the letter that helped describe their relationship. It included fruit, whipped cream, and several types of lewd and lascivious acts. (Strawberries would not have been my first choice here.) This was yet another woman who was told by her spouse that she was crazy.

Therefore the question begs to be asked: *Why would individuals put the details of their illicit relationships on a computer and then leave it stored there for others to find?* The answer varies, but the most common reasons are a false sense of security, a drastic misunderstanding of technology, and underestimating of a spouse's technical ability or their level of determination.

A High Level of Technical Skills Is Not Necessary

In most of my cases, spouses have had very limited technical ability, but their determination was the factor that led to their success. One woman had no technical skills, yet she hacked the voicemail of her husband's cell phone and began taping his incoming messages. Tell me she wasn't determined! From my experience, when a spouse is pushed to the limits and then told that they are crazy, watch out! They can and often will accomplish anything they set their mind to. Don't underestimate yourself. You can do this, and you will be successful.

In one case, I walked a client through the process of removing a laptop hard drive over the phone. She knew very little about computers. The amazing part was that she not only removed the hard drive, she also imaged the hard drive and sent the images to me for analysis. In her case, time was of the essence and I was not able to jump on a plane that day, yet the result was that the evidence was preserved, and we recovered all the data that she later used to help her make a decision.

Determination is a very strong force that can help us achieve even the most tedious tasks. In another case, for example, I met with a client in her office to discuss the potential for locating evidence on her home computer. While I was in her conference room, she showed me shredded pieces of a Post-it note and asked me if I knew someone who could put it back together. She stated that she saw her husband put the note into their home shredder, and she wanted to be able to see what was written on it. I felt that she was asking me to do it for her, but I also knew that I was too busy with numerous forensic cases and that I just did not have the time. I told her that I did not know anyone who could help. I could see the hurt in this woman's eyes and her need to know exactly what her husband was involved in. This is what made her so focused, so determined to see this through.

Toward the end of the case, I met with her again in her office to review our findings, which she was meticulously storing as she received them from our firm over the past few weeks. As I looked through the well-organized box of information she had amassed, I noticed a small piece of yellow paper sticking out from under one of the binders. I grabbed it by its corner and pulled it out. To my amazement, it was that Post-it note that had been shredded beyond repair – only, it was now meticulously taped together. It was one of the most pathetic looking pieces of paper that I had ever seen, but I could read every word on it. I looked at the note, then looked at her and asked, "Who did this for you?"

She responded, "I did. I needed to know."

I thought to myself, "Oh my God, I'm working with 007." I could only hope for her husband's sake that she did not have a license to kill. She never ceased to amaze me.

Cyber Lies is designed to give *you* the technological advantage, so you can be successful in preserving the evidence, gaining access to the information you need to make crucial decisions, and preventing you from making mistakes – or at least reducing the amount of mistakes you may make. Given today's unfortunate environment, you will need a tool that will enable you to follow up on your suspicions before you continue to invest time and other resources that so many people have ended up losing. It will help you to avoid situations like some of my clients, who found out too late that despite lies their spouses told them, their spouses had never been interested in having a family, and my clients were left in their forties and fifties having to start a new life without the prospect of achieving one of their important personal goals.

Work Hand-in-Hand with Your Lawyer

So the questions remain: *Are you prepared? Are you ready to do what it takes to find the truth?* In some cases, this journey may take you walking up to the line of what is legal and what is not, but making sure that you never cross that line. It is a line that changes from attorney to attorney, jurisdiction to jurisdiction, and judge to judge. It is a line that keeps moving as technology evolves. I mentioned earlier that women have hacked the voicemail system of their husband's cell phones, while other women have acquired their husband's personal laptop computers. Were these activities legal?

The answers may be different, based on circumstances and jurisdiction, so it is important to work with your lawyer. In the cases where the women acquired their husband's personal laptop computers, these actions were okayed by lawyers, who advised them that there was no problem acquiring a computer that was kept in the home. The only reason the husbands found out that their computers were accessed was because their wives confronted them with all the evidence of their infidelity. It turned out that the husbands were not only using the computers to surf porn sites during the day, but also to communicate with others using multiple online personalities on swapping, dating, and cheating sites for about three to six hours per day, five days a week.

Something important for you to know is that the opposing counsel will always claim that you have broken the law, even when your attorney has advised you that your actions are perfectly legal; so, be ready for that. I have been involved in many cases where it was clear that my clients had every legal right to image their spouse's computer, yet opposing counsel accused them of all types of criminal acts. It's a tactic they use to get you to back off and return the computer and the image files that you created. Don't! Ignore the comments of the opposing counsel, let your lawyer deal with them, and do what *your* lawyer tells you to do. It is easy to start to question yourself when you read such foolishness that your spouse's lawyer writes in letters that you are always copied on. Once you continue with your analysis, it may become all so clear why opposing counsel did not want you to see the contents of that hard drive. The evidence identified on that hard drive will serve as your vindication and the indictment of your spouse's character.

I want you to be successful, and I also want to make sure that you stay within the bounds of the law. Get your lawyer involved in all the aspects of your activities and do not make decisions by yourself. If your attorney gives you advice that the judge subsequently does not agree with, at least the judge knows that you based your actions on legal advice, and they may not hold that against you. Technology can not only challenge our legal system, but also frustrate us, so make sure you are prepared.

According to Vikki Ziegler, a prominent divorce attorney involved in many high-profile cases and the founder of DivorceDating.com, people need to be proactive in their litigation while working closely with their attorneys. She states, "In many ways, divorce is similar to death and is, in fact, the death of a present and future relationship. It is an emotional roller coaster that attacks you right in the heart and soul of the core of who you are. Being informed is the best tool you can provide yourself in protecting your emotional and financial well being."

Protecting Your Privacy

Now for the advice: *Be discreet.* Don't take this book home and read it in front of your spouse. I can almost hear the conversation right now.

Cheating Spouse: "Is this a new book? I don't remember seeing this on the Book-of-the-Month Club® listing."

Now when I say be discreet, I mean in all aspects of your computer forensic activities and divorce proceedings. On one occasion, an attorney gave their client a list of experts with whom the client could consult. The client kept the list in her purse, where her husband discovered it. Once he saw my name on that list, and read that I was a computer forensic expert, the computer suddenly disappeared from the house. Not good!

Let me take a minute to tell you the response that I typically get from a client when I advise them to take the steps necessary to protect their privacy: they usually tell me that it is not necessary. Clients who do this are falling into the same trap as their spouse because they have a false sense of security, a drastic misunderstanding of technology, and they are clearly underestimating their spouse's technical ability or their level of determination. Remember, I used these same words earlier in this chapter?

It's worth mentioning that when a spouse is cheating, they may become "suspicious" and very interested in finding out what you might know about their activities. Even if you are not aware of their curiosity, they may be looking at *your* actions very closely. They will often go through your purse or wallet, take a look at the computer for e-mail messages and Web content, examine your car, review your voicemail messages, go through the mail, and pull apart the garbage. Yes, they really do this. How do you think the husband that I mentioned earlier in the book found the list of experts? Don't fall into that same trap as your spouse and don't waste your money. You paid for this book, so take the advice and use it.

Dos and Don'ts

So here are some dos and don'ts. Some of these may not apply if you are not living with your spouse. That may not stop them from gaining access to crucial information, however, so make decisions wisely and leave nothing to chance.

✗ Don't give anyone (attorney or expert) your home phone number, or they may end up leaving you a message that will be discovered by your spouse. Use your cell phone to receive calls.

✗ Don't have any products or correspondence mailed to your home. Have them mailed to a post office box or sent to a friend's house. Even if your spouse no longer lives with you, they may drive by when you are not at home and review your mail.

✗ Purchase a document shredder if you do not have one and take the time to shred all important papers that you no longer plan to keep regarding your findings or communications between you and your attorney or expert. Never throw any important documents out in the garbage. Yes, spouses do look through the garbage.

✗ Never do any *research* on a computer that is kept in the home. Your spouse may review it when you are not at home and find out that you are contemplating divorce and/or researching computer forensics and data recovery.

✗ Once you receive a voicemail on your cell phone, delete the message so your spouse cannot get access to it. Also, delete the phone number from the INCOMING call log on your cell phone. If you don't, your spouse will be able to review that log each night when you are not paying attention and they will know with whom you are communicating.

✗ Don't make calls from your cell phone, as they will show up on the cell phone bill, which can then be accessed by your spouse. If you call your lawyer or a computer forensic expert from your cell phone, your spouse may find out about it and remove the computer from your home or cause important data to be deleted and overwritten. Please understand that although you may not be currently living with your spouse, if they are listed on the cell phone account, they will be able to gain access to that information by simply making a phone call to the provider.

If your spouse moves out, then make sure you call the cell phone provider and have your spouse removed from all accounts. If that is not possible, then have the phone number moved to a new account. Follow up with the cell phone company to make sure that this was accomplished.

✗   If you purchase software utilities or hardware suggested in any of the chapters of this book, make sure not to pay for them using your credit card. If you pay with a credit card, then your spouse may find out what you are up to and again the computer may disappear or be erased permanently.

If your spouse moves out, then make sure you call the credit card company and have your spouse removed from all accounts, or open new accounts.

✗   If you are planning to work at home performing computer forensics, make sure that your spouse is not going to be at home for several hours. Further, never store potential evidence at home.

✗   Change your work voicemail password, change your cell phone voicemail password, change your home message machine password, and change passwords for any and all e-mail accounts.

✗   Delete any old e-mail accounts and any messages that you no longer need. Make sure you check with your lawyer before deleting any information, however, as you do not want to be accused of intentional spoliation. Spoliation is the intentional deletion of potential evidence.

2

Infidelity

Understanding Infidelity

I have been involved in numerous divorce-related cases and have seen all sides, had access to all the facts, and have listened to the reasons that brought people to this point in their lives. Given today's moral climate and the disturbing changes in social trends, I felt it was necessary to include the topic of infidelity in my book. I have seen the pain that it causes and have often tried to help my clients through words of comfort and by directing them to get the professional help they need. Counseling is a very important aspect of dealing with infidelity. For that reason, don't gloss over this chapter. It has so much information that you can use immediately to help prepare you to search for the truth.

Infidelity is nothing new; it is almost as old as mankind. Infidelity is a difficult trend to track due to how technology and society have evolved over this past decade. For that reason, statistical figures vary based on whom and how the study was performed. The lack of clear definitions and the attempt to redefine social values and morals by liberals and conservatives alike has led to even greater confusion.

When then-President Bill Clinton stood before the American people and claimed that he did not have sex with Monica Lewinsky, it was the latest attempt to redefine sex as we knew it, and a movement grew behind the president to steer the country into a different direction. The Monica Lewinsky affair did not create the movement to redefine morals and values, but it certainly brought it to a new level that many media outlets used to springboard their agendas. So the questions remain: *Is oral sex infidelity? Is cyber sex infidelity?* Because the definition of infidelity varies from one person to another, there is no way to accurately measure infidelity trends.

According to Ruth Houston an estimated 50 to 70 percent of all men cheat on their spouses. While the percentage of women falls into a much lower category, the percentage has doubled in the past ten years. In other words, women are starting to catch up to men at alarming rates. Ruth Houston has been a journalist for over twenty years and has been researching and writing on infidelity for the past eleven years. Ruth herself has been a victim of infidelity and is the author of *Is He Cheating on You?: 829 Telltale Signs* (Lifestyle Publications, 2002). You can find additional information about this book at www.InfidelityAdvice.com. I highly recommend her book as another resource to use to better understand, plan, and cope with infidelity.

Ruth cited inaccurate surveys as one reason the infidelity numbers vary. She stated that you should never ask a cheater if they are cheating because the answer will always be no. Cheaters lie. They have created a separate life built by lies and they perpetuate that life by continuing to spin new lies. Cheaters don't cheat because of their spouses. They cheat for many reasons, but I can tell you that it is always because of their weaknesses – not yours.

Ruth Houston states that infidelity is one of the leading reasons for divorce, followed by financial problems, communication, and compatibility issues. Infidelity can occur for a number of reasons, which include a desire for more sex, a desire for a variety of sexual partners, sexual curiosity, the thrill of the chase, a need to feel special, sexual addiction, and opportunistic sex. For opportunistic sex, the individual may not be out looking for an affair, but is eager to participate if the chance comes up *and* they are confident they will not be caught.

You may be asking why so many people are cheating on their spouses. According to Ruth Houston, cheating on a spouse has been glamorized in the media. From TV programs to sensationalized headlines, infidelity is hot. The media is responsible for turning adultery into an adventure, making it exciting and positioning it as the moral climate of today. Headlines, media showcases, and rumors all told us that Prince Charles was cheating on Diana with Camilla. Ruth said that when Prince Charles married Camilla, it was a signal to other women that if you hang in there long enough, you may get the married prince of your dreams. This does not, however, excuse anyone for their reckless behavior; and the responsibility lies directly with each and every one of us to make the right decisions. Our destiny lies not in what we read or hear, but in the decisions that we make. Ruth writes that infidelity is not the fault of the faithful spouse. Regardless of what someone has done, it does not give their spouse a license to cheat.

The Internet is another reason for an adverse increase in the number of people cheating on their spouses. In the past, cheaters had to overcome a huge obstacle, which was to find others who also wanted to cheat. Years ago, cheating resulted in public humiliation, shame and being shunned by society; there was a stigma attached. Today, there is no stigma, and so-called entrepreneurs now provide Web portals dedicated to helping people cheat on their spouses. The Internet has become the new meat market of the new millennium.

I do not want to over simplify this, and I recognize that there are times when marriages end for a number of reasons. There may be many reasons that are acceptable for terminating a marriage, but it is never acceptable to leave one's spouse because of a desire for a variety of sexual partners. It is that simple. It may not be that *easy* to some people, but it is that *simple.* We set the parameters and create a situation that we try to fit right and wrong into. Right and wrong are not complex, but we have a habit of making it that way, and we do it to our advantage.

I recognize that there are times when two people who had not been searching for lovers find one another and fall in love. Sometimes, for example, if not for a series of unfortunate events, they might never have met. And because one helped the other during a traumatic time in their life, a bond started to grow that neither person could anticipate. I am not talking about opportunistic sex, but rather the way two people are bound by an emotion that forms into the love they feel for each other. Because it can lead to divorce, it is unfortunate when this takes place.

Further, although this is something I do not like to see happen, I do understand how two people can find themselves in this situation. When this occurs, it affects all the people involved. If the emotions and circumstances lead to an affair, then the faithful spouse is hurt. If no affair takes place, then both would-be lovers may suffer a depression that could last for some time as a result of their making the right decision.

What's the Attraction?

Dr. Luann Linquist says that "individuals involved in affairs experience both benefits and costs. Often the affair continues as long as the perceived benefits outweigh the costs." Dr. Linquist is an expert in relationships and provides information through her website www.DeleteStress.com. She has appeared on *Oprah, Geraldo, CNN, Hard Copy,* and *FOX,* and counsels people involved in affairs without judging them. I highly recommend that you read her book, *Secret Lovers,* to get another perspective on affairs and for suggestions on how to cope.

Dr. Linquist, while not promoting affairs, has done extensive research that reveals some of the perceived benefits of affairs, which include sexual and emotional satisfaction, new perceptions of the self, added dimensions to sex, body or personality changes, and a sense of being in charge. The costs, however, include guilt and pain, confusion and depression, loss of family/spouse, loneliness, a loss of reputation, and potential legal suits. In *Secret Lovers,* Dr. Linquist also states that often a person who ends up having an affair was not looking to engage in one. Many affairs begin with attraction that is at first not sexual, but includes components such as intellectual stimulation, strong personal or physical attraction, close emotional ties, and propinquity.

In my experience with divorce cases, I have found that personal or physical attraction can occur when two people work together, whether or not they work for the same company. The fact that they are working on the same project and share time together – even if it is only a few hours a week – is what matters. If the attraction is there, then the brief time they spend together can actually build their anticipation more rapidly than if they had spent much more time together. This fact can lead the two to enter an affair much quicker than they would have otherwise. Their attraction builds for any number of reasons, yet it is typically supported by the married person comparing their potential lover to their spouse. A woman might see a man she works with and wonder why her husband does not act like this great guy. A man might see a woman and wonder why his wife does not pay as much attention to him as his would-be lover does. While both perceptions might be accurate, they are viewed and skewed through rose-colored glasses.

The fact is that most people act differently when they are in a professional environment. This is the learned behavior that was ingrained in all of us from the time we were children. Remember many years ago when you were going out in public and your mom said, "Now don't embarrass me"? Every time we went out, our parents dressed us up and then threatened us to behave ourselves – or else. It is something that we all carry with us even today. Men and women take a tremendous amount of time to dress up and make sure that they look their best. We often start the night before, choosing our clothes, setting our alarm clocks, and planning out a day in order to make sure we look attractive at work. Others, though, may rush through everything and because of their charm and looks, it appears that they care more than they actually do. When you're driving to work, you can tell which people are running late. They're combing their hair, shaving, or putting on make up in the car. By the time they get to work, they look, feel, and act their best. It's not rocket science. It's human nature that they would be more attractive. If you were able to see how that particular person acted in a less-controlled environment, such as at their home, you would see a much different person. At home, we are more comfortable and we are less likely to dress and act our best. A husband comes home from work, taking off his tie as he is walking through the door. A woman walks through the door and kicks off those nice shoes, claiming that they are killing her feet. Then the complaints start. They tell their spouse all about their day and how tough it was. (Would they do that with their lover?) Then the pressures start from both sides. The other spouse shares details about their day with the kids. Both have financial concerns, as well as problems that affect all families. There is no doubt about the fact that when we are in a work environment, we are much different.

Close emotional ties often occur as two people share a struggle, help one another, or confide in each other. Since the bonds that occur from this interaction can be strong, this often leads to emotional infidelity and cause the individuals to have an affair, or even leave their spouses. I have seen emotional infidelity not only grow in the workplace, but also in online interaction – Web forums, blogs, and just about any online community site where people can meet, interact, and learn about each other. It may start out on a county Web forum making political statements or addressing an issue that is important to them. Then others delve into the mix with their opinions – some against, and some who side with your position. It can be the person who sides with them or the person who challenges them; either way, a communication link has been initiated and has a good possibility of growing. Neither person was looking to have an affair and chances are that, but for the Web forum, they would never have met.

In the workplace, the connection can be a project that they both share the burden to complete, an achievement that another person helps them to accomplish, or simply the social interaction that they share every day. *No matter how it happens, the connection allows an emotional tie to build, becoming strong enough to take the relationship to the next level.*

Opportunity is key in a few instances, such as in how people meet or how they interact; but it is most important in providing the ability for two people to have time alone where they can have an affair undetected. A county Web forum provides an opportunity for the two people to meet. The workplace provides the opportunity for two people to interact. But opportunity goes far beyond that. It is often professional conferences and business trips that provide a venue not only to grow a relationship, but to bring it to the next level, whether or not they are aware that this is occurring.

Relationships can blossom at conferences where two people have time to spend with each other and share unique learning experiences that they have a passion for. It might be a certification course for a professional license or a technology show debuting the newest devices that can be pertinent to your industry. Two people can browse the show while having a great time. The show then ends in the late afternoon or early evening and both agree to meet for dinner. Having dinner with a member of the opposite sex is not a problem. Remember, it's a business trip and they are meeting to discuss business – at least that is what most of us would rationalize. While both people may try to convince themselves that nothing is going to happen, it is the environment that will help push the relationship along. A shared passion, soft music, good food, and alcoholic beverages made available in most restaurants, all work to relax them and lower their inhibitions. It might be at this conference or it might be at the next, but the opportunity to have an affair is present. It is one kiss away from the obvious next step, which is a walk to the other person's room.

Why You Need to Know

A few people have told me that this book would be responsible for ending more marriages than it saves and that a spouse does not have a right to know about the private life of their spouse. In fact, one publicist refused to help promote this book for that very reason. She stated that it was against her corporate philosophy to promote my book.

First things first: It was never an objective of this book to save marriages. That decision can only be made by the two people involved in that marriage. Further, it is important to remember that it was the actions of one of the two people that created an unstable marriage in the first place – not this or any other book. The objective of this book is to show the faithful spouse how to find, recover, and analyze information that is stored on computers or cell phones in order to make decisions. That's it, and it is that simple.

My pundits will ask, *Why does the faithful spouse need to know?* The answer is not complex, but there are several reasons. I have been involved in many divorce cases and have had few cases where the cheating spouse is dating only one person. The majority of the cases involve the cheating spouse dating multiple people, the growing trend today. Either way, a cheating spouse often creates a trail of potential evidence located on a variety of technological devices that can easily be accessed and reviewed. However, the more people your spouse is involved with, the more information will be available for your review. The reason for this is that individuals involved with multiple people take part in more activities that are responsible for leaving telltale signs and creating multiple data formats that leave a trail of their activities on a variety of technological devices. It might be Web cache that reveals they are surfing dating or cheating sites. It may be text-messages or pictures on a cell phone that document their infidelity. Or, it may be EZPass records that prove they were not where they told you they were. Whatever the reason, you need to know if your spouse is involved with other people for several reasons. First and foremost, for health reasons. When an unfaithful spouse is sexually active with one or more partners, they expose the faithful spouse to communicable and potentially incurable diseases. The faithful spouse needs this information to make crucial decisions, whether that decision is to use protection when having sex with their spouse, to stop having sex with their spouse altogether, or to potentially leave their spouse. The fact is that without this information, the faithful spouse is placed in a high health-risk category that could have been avoided. When the unfaithful spouse made the decision to sleep with multiple partners, they accepted the potential risks. Whether or not they really thought it through does not matter. They made a conscious decision to accept the risk. However, if the unfaithful spouse does not inform their spouse that they are doing so, they are taking away that same opportunity for that spouse to make their choice. The actions of the unfaithful spouse then expose their spouse to danger, which is unconscionable.

The faithful spouse also needs the information to help make a determination about their financial future. For example, if the faithful spouse has been a stay-at-home mom and finds out that her husband is involved with another person or multiple people, she needs to be able to anticipate the possibility that her husband will leave. This is important information to help her realize that she needs to start to make a plan. The faithful spouse could start to develop a skill, return to school to build a career, apply for employment, apply for credit instruments, and identify all marital assets and help protect her portion. All of these actions would help support her and any children going forward. The end result is that they would not be caught unprepared and adapt quicker to the unfortunate change in their life.

If you go to any one of the major search engines and perform a Web search using the keywords "secret divorce planning," you will see several links that provide information marketed to men and women who are planning a divorce. It appears that several links have the same goal, which is to get their clients a better settlement than their spouses get. I have several problems with some of these products. First, the term "secret planning" implies that you want to gain the upper hand and leave your spouse totally unprepared with the result of your planned actions. Anyone who would do that to another person they once loved and shared their most intimate moments with is lower than the scum on the bottom of algae that lies on the ocean floor. In other words, when you leave your spouse, their life has instantly been made better by your absence. I understand the need to plan, but not to leave your spouse in an unprepared state to their disadvantage. I will never understand how anyone – either men or women – could do any of this to their spouse. Some of these links provide information including topics such as increasing the family debt now, unprofitable businesses help, how to get big alimony payments from your husband, how to make him pay your legal expenses, how to win by acting, moving assets out of the home, and how to dig up information and use it to "screw" your spouse. Have we finally arrived at the point in our civilization where we *Do unto others before they do unto you?* Remember, it's not society; it's you who makes the decisions that you have to live with. I hope no matter who you are, you do what you know in your heart is right.

I recognize that there are times when you may be dealing with a spouse who does not play fair, who may be a horrible person – and you have to do what is necessary to survive. I have seen that. I had one case where the husband towed his wife's only car away – and she was a stay-at-home mom. He later told her to find a boyfriend to buy her a car because he had purchased a car for his girlfriend. In another case, the husband was stealing money out of the kids' bank accounts. Whatever you have to do, I believe that the deciding point should be when you ask yourself, *Did I do what is right?*

The faithful spouse also needs the information to help them come to grips with the fact that their spouse does not have the same life objectives. For example, if the faithful spouse had been planning to start a family and it is apparent that the other had no plans or desires to reach that goal, it might prove crucial to the faithful spouse to know this. In a few of my cases, this is exactly what happened. The wives in these cases were distraught because it became evident that after having spent so many years with their husbands, they suddenly found out that their husbands never wanted children, although the wives did. They stated that if they had known this, they would not have continued the marriage. One excuse after another kept them hanging in there when their husbands were lying to them the whole time.

Finally, the spouse needs to collect the information necessary that proves that their spouse is actually involved in an affair. They need this information in order to confront their cheating spouse. Almost every relationship expert agrees that the faithful spouse needs to confront the cheating spouse. You cannot just simply ignore the issues that face and affect you every day. However, you must do two things before you confront them. First, you must plan to ensure that you are able to leave if you do not feel that the marriage is worth saving. Second, you need to collect the proof necessary that will show them you really know what is going on.

In most of my cases, it was the man who was cheating on his wife with multiple women. While the numbers are growing for women, it is still men who more often than not are leading such despicable lives. I am not talking about when a married man falls in love with another woman, I am talking about the sexual perversion that occurs when men sleep with multiple women in one week, and it is all about sex and not the relationships. There is absolutely no similarity between this behavior and the intimacy that is typically shared between men and women. As a man, I am embarrassed when I see men act this way. I see the devastation it can lead to. Some men need to learn what it means to be a real man.

I have to leave you here, as I am not the one who can tell you how to confront your cheating spouse. I can tell you how and where to find data on technological devices because that is my expertise. I mentioned two very good books earlier in this chapter, and I highly recommend that you purchase them. Each provides a very different perspective that I believe you can learn from.

Potential Signs of Infidelity

When anyone is involved in a new relationship, it's human nature to exhibit any one of a number of characteristics that serve as telltale signs that reflect the change in our lives. This change is not always noticeable by people who do not know you well, but it is very evident to those who see you regularly.

This is also the case when married people become involved with people outside the marriage. This change is not only in the way they behave, but may also be a change in their daily activities. The first people to notice these changes are usually the spouses, although at first it will not be clear to them what these changes mean. They often think that what they see is odd and out of character, but will usually shrug it off until they start to notice other changes. It is at this point that they will become concerned. Any one of these changes individually does not mean that your spouse is involved in an affair; although as changes in their daily routine continue to increase, the likelihood that your spouse is involved in an extramarital affair or affairs increases dramatically.

The traditional changes in behavior include a noticeable improvement in grooming, starting to work out, working longer hours, losing interest in sex with you, losing interest in family activities, paying more attention to you and pointing out your faults, becoming defensive when you ask questions about their day, starting fights over trivial matters, lying about where they have been, starting to pry into your daily routine, and starting to ask you questions about why you're curious. Remember that spouses who cheat are very suspicious and they will be just as curious about your activities as you are about theirs.

All of these behavioral changes are typical and very predictable. These changes in how your spouse acts and behaves are clear telltale signs that something is going on in their lives and only you will be able to determine what that is. You know them the best and only you can decipher the meaning. It is important to note that your spouse may not know that they are exhibiting these signs. If you notice the changes, do not bring them to your spouse's attention or they may start to become aware of their behavior and make modifications. This will make it harder for you to detect the differences. Start to keep a record of these changes, compare these to other changes you notice, and you will see a pattern start to emerge.

In addition to the changes in their behavior, they may also change their activities, especially relating to technology. Individuals involved in inappropriate activity will often spend an increased amount of time online. That is not to say that all people who spend an enormous amount of time online are guilty of cheating or surfing for porn. You have to judge your spouse based on what you know about them. You need to ask yourself, *Has my spouse always spent this much time on the computer, or is this new?* Remember, you are looking for changes in their behavior or activities. You are not trying to match their normal behavior or activities to a profile. It is the *change* that should raise your suspicions, not their usual activity.

When these individuals are online at home, they will either close the door to the room or rearrange the computer so they are facing the door. This will place the monitor away from the view of the door and the spouse will have plenty of time to change the screen if their spouse walks into the room. They also will stay on the computer for a very long amount of time, including into the early-morning hours while their spouse sleeps.

Despite the fact that their online usage has increased, you will not see much Internet history because they are deleting it on a regular basis. A cheating spouse will be very protective about the computer and claim that deleting Web history and Web cache has everything to do with privacy or stopping viruses and preventive maintenance. In addition, your spouse may install a software product that is designed to delete Web cache and log files that typically document a user's online activity. The presence of the software utility by itself is not nefarious, but may be if it has been installed recently. If you know how to check the installation date of the software product, then do so and make sure you record it. If you do not know, then you will by the time you read this entire book.

You might notice that there are separate logins for you and your spouse when there was only one in the past. This is because they do not want you to have access to what they have access to. When you create two separate logins, you create two separate profiles on the computer and all history, Web cache, and just about everything else is stored in separate PROFILE folders. However, most of the time, the spouse has a total misunderstanding of technology and operating system security and you can get access to what you need with absolutely no effort at all. Even when the spouse knows what they are doing, there are simple ways to bypass the operating system security. This will be covered later in the book.

The spouse may start to spend time in online community sites and they may even install a computer camera for when they are involved in online chats. This should be a big tip that something else may be going on. Again, a computer camera in and of itself is not nefarious, but if it is in addition to other activities that I mentioned earlier, that should raise your level of suspicion.

They will be very protective of their cell phone. They will go outside or move to a remote section of the house to take certain cell phone calls. They will carry the phone with them and not place it down except when they go to sleep, and they may delete the INCOMING or OUTGOING phone logs on a daily basis. Even if you don't see the entire phone logs deleted, they may be deleting individual phone calls so they do not show up in the INCOMING or OUTGOING phone logs. While this is harder to detect, it is not impossible to detect. This will be covered later in the book. In addition, their cell phone usage will skyrocket from the norm. Although you may not see much more activity as far as calls outbound, there will be an increased amount of inbound calls. This is because they may be using that cell phone as their home or work phone number for their online personalities. In other words, they may be misleading people that they meet online by telling them that the phone number is their home number. Today, more and more people are more apt to check things out before they go on a date with someone they meet online. Sometimes that check includes a call to the person's home to make sure they are not married; but most people are not savvy enough to realize they are calling a cell phone. If you call your spouse's cell phone and their outgoing message begins with, "Sorry I'm not home right now," then something is up.

There are plenty of free online resources and other sites that charge a fee to find out who a specific number belongs to. These are called reverse lookups because we typically attempt to find a person's phone number by looking up their name and address. A reverse lookup is when we attempt to find a person's name and address by looking up their phone number. All you have to do is do a Web search using your favorite search engine. Then, use the keywords "cell phone reverse lookup," or "reverse lookup" for line telephones. (Our typical home and work phones are referred to as line phones because there is a phone company line that is attached to our home or work building that provides phone service.)

It may seem that there is a lot to learn, but you have a lot at stake. The information in this book is not difficult and the Internet provides a host of resources that might help you going forward. This book is geared to encourage readers to find and use the free resources available on the Internet, whether that resource is an online service or software application. Remember, free is better than cheap. Use this book to obtain a good understanding of technology and identify what you need to accomplish. Then develop a strategy to move forward. You can find help with the variety of resources identified in this book, as well as many other online services that you can identify with just a few keyword searches using your favorite search engine. Remember, you can do this.

3

Infidelity and the Internet

Internet Dating

The Internet is a great resource, one that provides instant access to the information that you are looking for. The best part, of course, is that there are no fees other than the connection to your home or business. There are several ways to connect to the Internet. We can dial into a local Internet provider offering dial-up service using a modem on our computer. We can connect via a DSL or cable connection provided to our home or business from a local provider. Finally, we can access it wirelessly at home using a wireless router, or while we are in the middle of a park using a broadband wireless carrier. We're familiar with many features of the Internet, but there are growing trends relating to it that you need to know about. These trends include cheating spouses using legitimate services provided by major corporations to support and further their illicit activities. In addition, there are companies that provide services with the specific intention of helping your spouse cheat on you.

The Internet connects us to people and information, including one of the fastest-growing services offered – providing access to individuals interested in dating. Many of these great services enable and foster relationships that might never have occurred a few short years ago. While the services vary, many sites offer access to participants' pictures, bios, and personality assessments, making it easy for you to browse and locate potential dating prospects without even signing up for membership. You simply go to the dating services site, fill in certain criteria such as sex, age, and city/state/country of the person you would like to meet, and instantly a list of potential candidates and their pictures pop up, with a brief bio for each person. Not bad, if you are single and looking to use the Internet to meet new people.

These sites, however, are often preyed upon by individuals who are married (and mostly men), who are providing not only bogus information about their marital status, but even about their identity. While I am sure that there are some single people interested in dating married people to avoid any long-term commitment, most of the people who use dating sites for singles expect to meet people who are, in fact, *unmarried.* By the way, in most cases *dating* is not the intention of the married spouse who uses these dating sites to meet people. Further, single sites have started a campaign to weed out and even prosecute married people posing as singles. While I do not really see how the sites can legally accomplish that, it is a start in the right direction. It has had an effect on those who sign up, as there has been a noticeable reduction in the amount of married people signing up as single on these dating sites. However, married people were not the only ones who noticed this trend and the demand that it created.

A New Market Emerges

Enterprising individuals saw the impact on these displaced married men and found a solution to solve the business problem. It was simple: Create a site and provide supporting services that would help married men and women find people to cheat with. Now I know what you are going to say: *WHAT THE HELL IS GOING ON?* Welcome to the Internet and the new world of depravation. Please buckle your seat belts because it gets a lot worse. What do you expect when we live in a world where the Internet provides software that turns your cell phone into a personal vibrator? One site states, "Women everywhere are discovering how to harness the vibrations of their cell phones for pleasure. Learn how to dial yourself up an off-the-hook orgasm." And another site states, "Unlock the hidden pleasures in your mobile phone with the Purring Kitty!" It will have to be a real emergency before I borrow anyone's cell phone again.

Cheating sites are springing up everywhere, including sites such as AshleyMadison.com, Meet2Cheat.com, Discreet-Adventures.com, MarriedCafe.com, and MarriedSecrets.com – just to name a few. The sites don't beat around the bush, they are right up front about everything: *They are here to help you cheat on your spouse.* So I decided to interview one of the individuals involved with the operation side of a cheating site who agreed to the interview. They provided what I consider to be a unique insight to the industry as a whole.

The Ashley Madison Agency hosts a Web portal that provides a series of services to married people. Their Web address is www.AshleyMadison.com and their website states that their operation is located in Toronto, Canada. I spoke to one of their founders by the name of Darren Morgenstern, who serves as Director of Operations for the Ashley Madison Agency. Mr. Morgenstern stated that the Ashley Madison Agency was founded to meet a market that already existed. Their corporate motto, "When monogamy becomes monotony," was chosen as a catchy phrase to sum up their offerings, and it does just that. The founder of AshleyMadison.com provided some unique insight into why people cheat on their spouses. His take on this issue is that cheating on your spouse is not a matter of gender, but a matter of opportunity.

Morgenstern stated that more men are in the work environment meeting with other professionals on a regular basis and, therefore, have a much greater opportunity to cheat on their spouses. He also added that as more women have returned to the workforce, their infidelity numbers have increased.

There is no doubt about the fact that people are much different animals in the work environment than they are at home. Professionals often dress their best for work, act their best, and are more likely to be polite and much nicer than they are at home. It's not their intent to treat their spouses with less respect, it is just that they are more comfortable in their homes and therefore act differently. In other words, their behavior is less appealing in their home than it is in a work environment. This makes them more attractive to the opposite sex while they are at work.

Morgenstern told me that a woman in the workplace looks at a man and judges him much differently than she does her husband. All she can think of is how her husband behaves at home and, therefore, this guy she sees every day at work is Prince Charming. If she only had a chance to compare notes with his wife, she would find out that he is much the same as her husband. We all act differently when we are at home than we do at work. It is human behavior to unwind at home and act more relaxed. We are not on guard or on our best behavior, the way we are in a professional environment.

Morgenstern further stated that there is a huge appetite in this industry from both men and women, but he conceded that men are the dominate users. In fact, the Ashley Madison Agency membership consists of about 85 percent men and 15 percent women. The median age is thirty-six, but the average age for females is from twenty-eight to thirty-nine years old and the average age for men is between thirty and forty-four years old. The Web portal starts off as a free service and then there are fees to increase your ability to meet and have encounters with people who interest you. He said that about 12 percent of men actually purchase an upgrade in membership services, which is drastically different from the 1.5 percent of women who purchase an upgrade. In addition, 5 percent of men seek gay encounters, while 5 percent of women seek lesbian encounters.

The Ashley Madison Agency has been in business for about four years and has seen its revenues double each year. Business is generated mostly through print ads, as well as radio and TV, and 10 percent of revenues come from affiliate programs (or where other websites have links, or refer Internet surfers to the Ashley Madison site). For the affiliate programs, traffic is tracked; and if the Internet surfer purchases a membership in the Ashley Madison program, the referring site is given a commission.

Morgenstern's position is that "We provide a safe forum for people to explore their feelings." To some, it is an environment where people can be more honest about their circumstances and deal with other people who are like-minded. However, I believe that in this industry there is very little honesty, especially to the spouses of individuals who frequent cheating sites. It appears that the goal is to be honest with people you don't know, but to intentionally deceive the one you love, potentially exposing them to danger.

The Ashley Madison Agency provides mail, messaging, and real-time chat, which segregates a member's online life from their real-world existence. Morgenstern insisted that the company is hands-off when it comes to helping people cheat. "We leave you with your own devices, and you must already know how to carry on an affair. We will not tell you how to take lipstick off your collar, but we will provide safety tips."I believe, however, that by providing a portal and support services specifically designed to help people cheat, these sites are enabling, supporting, and furthering the act of infidelity. This is a trend that is growing, and more and more people are now getting involved in portals such as the Ashley Madison Agency.

Web Services that Support Infidelity

There are also legitimate companies that offer services, both free and paid, that are utilized by individuals involved in affairs. These services are used to help support and further cheating activities. It is important to stress that most of these companies often do not know what their services are being used for, while others know full well. This makes it harder for the good spouse to find out and places them at a disadvantage for many obvious reasons. These services include anonymous e-mail accounts, Web forums, IP phones, and even a network of people who are willing to provide an alibi for you should your spouse become suspicious.

Almost all service providers offer free e-mail accounts that do not require you to provide a form of identification, and you can register using any name and designate your gender however you wish. So you can have multiple free e-mail accounts at Yahoo!®, MSN™, Google™, or any one of the hundreds of sites that offer these free services. All of these portals provide tremendous services, but not all are aware what these accounts are being used for. The way the services are designed allows anyone to create a fictitious online virtual personality.

Web forums provide us with the ability to set up an online profile complete with a picture, as well as a listing of our likes and dislikes. We can then opt in on their social community in order to meet others interested in discussion boards, dating, or just sex. Some offer other services that enable us to receive e-mail and voicemail messages. They are feature-rich sites that cheating spouses use to support and further their infidelity.

There are also payment services that are offered by legitimate companies that enable cheaters to disguise their online activity. For example, an individual involved in cheating or other inappropriate online activities, might place a certain amount on account with one of the popular payment gateways using their credit card. Then they use that payment service to pay for access to a dating site, cheating site, or other types of sites that they do not want their spouse to learn about. Keep an eye out on the credit card statements for these types of charges.

If your spouse gives you the phony excuse that they use a certain payment service because they do not like to conduct online transactions with their credit card, in most cases they are being disingenuous. This is because they have to use their credit card online to place the credit on their account with that payment gateway. Isn't that what they told you they did not like to do? Always watch for inconsistencies, ask them for the statements, and see what they say.

I do want to point out that payment gateways don't know – or even care – what their gateways are used for, and they are not doing anything wrong. Does a major credit card company care if someone uses their credit card to pay for a hotel to be with their significant other? No. Remember, it is your spouse who may be doing something wrong, not any of the companies that offer any of these services.

IP phones are devices that anyone can purchase with any area code and exchange they want. These phones operate using the Internet as a communication backbone. For example, you can purchase an IP phone, request an area code for Washington DC (202), and then ask for any exchange (the first three numbers after the area code) so it looks like you live in that area. When you have the phone plugged in on your home network in the state of New York, it rings there. If you have it plugged in on your work network in Connecticut, it rings there. And, if you have it plugged in using your hotel cable connection in California, it rings there. This is important to remember: *No matter where you are in the world, most times the caller ID will show you are in the 202 area.* Now, a cheating spouse can make it look like they are exactly where they want others to think they are – regardless of whether they are dialing out or receiving calls.

The alibi network allows members to vouch for the (fictitious) whereabouts of other members. Here is the way an alibi network works. Suppose a member tells his wife that he was at a vendor party meeting with clients on Monday evening. He will give his wife the name "Robert Smith," along with a phone number for Smith. When his wife calls Smith to verify her husband's activities on Monday evening, Smith will tell her that her husband was at the party and was pestering him all night trying to sell products to his company. Smith, though, may never have met her husband and certainly hadn't been at a vendor party on Monday evening. Alibi networks are set up for cheating spouses to cover their tracks and get away with deception. Deceit is paramount to cheating spouses, and there is often no level to which they will not stoop.

How Online Cheating Works

It will be important for you to know how a cheating spouse does what they do online and why. First, they will set up multiple online accounts using multiple online personalities. For example, they may have several e-mail accounts set up with multiple providers such as MSN, AOL™, Yahoo!, Google, or Hotmail, while using different names at each of these providers, such as Joe, Robert, Sam, and Alice. Why "Alice" if your spouse is a male? Men will often set up accounts using female names and use those accounts as references for other women.

So, if Joe is online communicating with a woman by the name of Jane Doe, they can tell Jane about Alice. If and when Jane contacts Alice by e-mail asking what kind of guy Joe is, Alice – who is really Joe – will write back with an excellent review. If Jane never contacts Alice, then

Alice might write to Jane saying that she has noticed that she is communicating with Joe in one of the discussion forums and that Joe is a really great guy. Is it that easy? Yes it is! It is not that women are naïve; we are all naïve when it comes to technology and to what extent people will go to in order to deceive us. Remember, deceit is the cornerstone of the cheater's world.

Men who cheat with multiple women also use the accounts to pose as women to interact with other women in order to plant the seed that they should engage in a threesome. It is their belief that if the request or suggestion originates from a female, then the woman would be more open to engage in a threesome.

Let's walk through the process of setting up multiple online accounts. It will be an eye-opening experience if you are not familiar with how it is accomplished. You will see how easy it is to pose as anyone you want. I should also tell you that faithful spouses use the same process to set up sting operations to trap their cheating spouses in their online activities. I would caution you on this and make sure that you are comfortable in taking part in this type of activity because there are a few things you need to accomplish in order to be successful. You must be able to maintain your composure when working undercover and interacting with your spouse. Also, you must understand the technologies involved and you must have a full understanding of the sites on which you are trying to interact with your spouse. Remember what I said at the beginning of the book: *Don't rush things.* You will get there and you will be successful if you take your time to learn what you need to know.

I am going to start with Yahoo! because that was the very first search engine established on the Internet.

1) Open your browser. Typically this is Internet Explorer™, but it may be Mozilla FoxFire®, or any one of a number of others. Go to www.yahoo.com.

2) When you get to the search engine, you can't help but notice **YAHOO!** written in red at the top left side of the page. (It should be noted that while the Yahoo! logo is usually colored in red, the

color and design of the wording changes to fit holidays and other special events.) You will then notice the word **Mail** also at the top of the page with the picture of an envelope just above it. This is actually an icon (picture) that you can click on.

3) **Click** on the word **Mail** and it will take you to the **Mail** page.

4) On the right side of the page, you'll notice a yellow rectangular box with the wording **Sign up for Yahoo! Click** on that yellow box and it will take you to a page where you can start to enter personal information for your new e-mail account.

If you actually read the terms and conditions of the account, you are required to provide true, accurate, and current information about yourself. Yahoo! takes no technical steps to enforce compliance with this policy and requires no confirmation about your true identity prior to granting you access to the account other than stating it in their policy. This is the same for most portals. If you request a user name that is already in use, Yahoo! also has a unique feature that will help you find a similar user name that is not in use.

All the information a cheater supplies is often false or at least misleading. In most of the cases that I have been involved in, cheating spouses lie about everything, including their real name, what they do for a living, and where they live. It is possible, too, that they supply real information that is false. For example, they may provide a home phone number that is directed to a service where a voicemail always picks up. They will make the recording sound like a home message, but it will be a service and you will not know. They might also have an IP phone that we discussed earlier and tell you that it is their work number, when in fact it is not. So remember, just because you get what appears to be real information does not mean the person is telling you the truth. Technology helps support the lies of cheaters.

5) Once you complete the Yahoo! form, you will then be able to login and you are ready to send and receive e-mail using that

account. It's that easy. It should take you less than two minutes to get your account operational. I want you to know right now that although I told you that you will be totally *anonymous,* that does not mean that the e-mail you send can't be traced – because it can.

Now you have successfully set up your first account. Next, set up another e-mail account at any one of the other sites that I mentioned earlier in this chapter. Then test the e-mail between accounts. I hope you realize that I brought you through this process so you can see first-hand how cheating spouses do this.

The next thing a cheating spouse would do is to get involved in online community Web forums, online personals, dating sites, and even cheating sites. Almost every major search engine and Web portal offers some of these services. If you open your browser again and go to www.yahoo.com, I will show you where the Yahoo! online personals are located and you can see the way it works.

1) Below the large red **YAHOO!** you will notice a bluish rectangle box. The menu options are in alphabetical order, so if you scan through the options, you will see the word **Personals. Click** on that link and it will take you to the **Yahoo! Personals** page. You can also get to this site by just typing in the following URL: http://personals.yahoo.com. There are also many other great sites, which include Match.com, eHarmony.com, Dating.com, and DivorceDating.com – just to name a few. These sites provide legitimate dating services to single or divorced people and all of them are worth checking out.

2) Once you get to the **Yahoo! Personals** page, it will be evident what you need to do in order to obtain a listing of eligible people to date. Go ahead in fill in the criteria and **Click** on the **Search** button. You need to do this yourself so you know exactly what your spouse may be doing. Notice that you will see small pictures of each of the people listed. These are referred to as thumbnail pictures.

3) You can actually go from page to page by **Clicking** on the **Next** button at the bottom right and see additional pages of photo listings. Notice the size of these pictures, notice that most of these individuals are posed, and that they are often dressed to impress.

Why are these thumbnail pictures important? Before I answer that question, I have another question that I want to ask you: *Did you take any action to download any of these images?* Your answer should be no, but all of the images that you just viewed are on your hard drive. The reason they are on your hard drive is because the browser that you are using caches all graphic images to your hard drive, which means they were downloaded onto your hard drive to make better use of bandwidth. Did you ever notice that when you go to a site for the first time, it appears to load slowly? Then when you return, the page just seems to jump up quickly. The reason is the images do not have to be downloaded again because they are on your hard drive. These images are stored in your USER PROFILE folder, which is located in the DOCUMENTS AND SETTINGS folder. In your USER PROFILE folder is another sub-folder titled TEMPORARY INTERNET FILES. All cached data is stored in that folder. If you were to review all the images in that folder, you would see the very images that you saw online. *How* to view the images will be covered later in the book. The important thing to remember right now is *what* they look like so when you see them on the computer that your spouse uses, you will know what they mean. The presence of hundreds of these files typically means that someone has spent a lot of time browsing dating or cheating sites. You need to do your homework by getting the experience necessary to access these files. This is the only way you will be able to determine what the information means when you find it.

I have to caution you not only on where you do your research, but on what computer. I will mention this several times because it is very important to remember: *Never do any work on the computer that you want to image or analyze.* There are a few reasons for this. If you use the computer you want to analyze, then it might be your Internet activity that is placing the images on the hard drive, and it may not be your spouse's activity at all. In addition, as you go from site to site, the browser is downloading new data to that computer's hard drive and this would overwrite deleted areas of the hard drive that you may want to search and recover. You also do not want to do this type of research on a computer that you use all the time, as your spouse may be looking at your computer and think that you are cheating on them. This is why it is best to use a computer at a friend's house, especially if they are single. There is a lot to remember so make sure to keep notes on the important points.

Once you are able to determine what site the files are from, you will be able to go online and see if your spouse's profile is in their dating site listing. Now for a question to see if you can apply what you learned so far: *How would you determine what dating or personals sites your spouse had been visiting?* Be honest and stop right here. If you think you have a good answer or if you can't think of anything, then proceed to the next paragraph.

The answer is Web cache, the graphic files located in the TEMPO-RARY INTERNET FILES folder under each PROFILE folder. Remember that big red YAHOO!? It is a graphic file. How about the **Mail** icon? That is a graphic file as well. All graphic files are cached to the hard drive and stored in the USER PROFILE by the browser. If you view the Web cache, then you will see other graphic files that belong to all the sites your spouse has been visiting, including porn sites, dating sites, and cheating sites. There are some obstacles that you might have to overcome, but most times it is right there to find if you just know where to look.

A few of the obstacles include security issues. Depending on how the system is configured and what security level you have been assigned, you might not have access to **View** or **Copy** the Web cache for review. However, you will learn how to get around that later in the book. Another obstacle is the ability of your spouse to delete the Web cache and Web history, but I will show you how to undelete the data. The last obstacle that I will mention is the ability of your spouse to install and use a software product designed to shred and overwrite deleted data. If this occurs, you will not be able to access that data. However, all is not quite lost.

I have had cases where spouses have installed shredding utilities, but after a while they became lazy in using the utility. This left day's and even week's worth of Web cache and history on the hard drive to be recovered. The point is, just because you see that an overwriting utility has been installed does not mean there is no data left on the hard drive. Don't assume anything, or you may regret it. Act like the utility is not there and proceed as you would have. Please, don't panic and don't give up. Besides, there are other types of data that an overwriting utility would not erase and this topic will be covered later in the book.

I have been told by a few of my clients that their spouses have deleted all the data and some have brought their computers to my business location to ensure that there was nothing left on the hard drive. While it took some convincing, all of my clients allowed me to access their hard drives and all of the cases resulted in finding information that revealed that their spouses were involved in other relationships. The point of this story is: *Never assume the worst and never give up.* Even if they delete the Web cache and then use a shredding utility to overwrite the deleted areas of the hard drive, a portion of their Web activity is also kept in the REGISTRY, which will survive because it is located in a protected system file. This file can be later accessed and reviewed.

Now that you have a sense for what sites your spouse may be visiting, it is time to visit those sites and try to see if you can locate a site profile that they may have setup. A site profile is personal information about them that they wish to share in order to attract others. It may or may not include a picture. It is referred to as a site profile, because it is used only at that specific site.

You know your spouse, so you would have to provide certain search criteria that might find them easily. If they lied about their age, what would be the lowest age they could get away with? Then use that age range. If they lied about their weight or what they did for a living, what would they say in a dating profile? All of this could be different based on the dating site you were searching. It is important for you to know this information so when you start to review Web history and other data, it will make more sense to you and you will have a better understanding of what is going on. It also will help you determine where to look for information based on what you see.

There are some other free Web services that you need to know about: Instant-messengers and free software used to make free and untraceable long distance calls. Let's start with instant-messengers.

Instant-messenger is a software product that you install on a computer and you can type in real-time to another person. When you use an instant-messenger program, the process of using it is referred to as IM'ing. So you could tell someone that "I will IM [eye-M] you later when I get home," and you would be using the term correctly. When you start the program, it typically displays a split screen. One portion of the screen is designed for you to type what you want to say to the other person and the other portion of the screen is designed to display the instant replies from the person you are communicating with. It is a real-time communication tool.

IM is versatile to use. It includes short message slang that is evolving every day. LOL, for example, is "Laughing Out Loud" in the majority of cases, but it has also been used to mean "Lots of Love." CUL8R is "See You Later." And for those of you who have kids, P911 means that parents are in the room and POS means that parents are looking over my shoulder. If you later find a slang term and you do not know what it means, just go to your favorite search engine and do a keyword search; for example, **im acronym pos.** Try it and you will see what you get back. Search engines will be your number one online resource for identifying things you need to know or make sense of – and they are absolutely free. You just need to understand how to use them to get the information you need.

If you type, "Hi, how are you feeling today?" the other person might type back, "I'm fine but work was hectic today." Some people have been known to IM for hours. IM'ing is very popular, especially between lovers because they think it is safer than e-mail. While this may be true to some extent, IM messages can be logged by one of the people involved in the IM communication or even unintentionally cached to the hard drive and potentially recovered later on. Cached means that the application has temporarily stored the IM message contents on the hard drive, much like caching the graphic images, as we discussed before. This cache is not stored in a folder, but lies in the unallocated areas of the hard drive. There is a chance that the messages may be overwritten and, then again, they may not be overwritten. The file system of the computer manages and keeps track of all the files that are a part of the file system. When a file is deleted, it is no longer considered to be part of the file system. In addition, while cached data is temporarily stored on the hard drive, it is also not part of the file system. The areas that these data reside on the hard drive is referred to as the unallocated portion of the hard drive. It is referred to as *unallocated* because the file system has not allocated that part of the hard drive for its files and it is not protected by the file system. Searching, reviewing, and recovering data located in the unallocated portion of the hard drive will be discussed later.

The application also provides the ability to log all IM communication, and either party may be doing just that. The log will show exactly who said what and at what time. I have seen disgruntled lovers store these communications in logs for use at a later time. When their lover does not end up leaving their spouse as promised, then the logs are sent to their home to help the process along.

The faithful spouse will often use the logging feature when they are working undercover trying to find out what their spouse is up to. Then, they will use that log as proof to confront their cheating and later on as evidence during a potential divorce proceeding. Once they start interacting with their cheating spouse, who does not know that they are communicating with their spouse, the faithful spouse will log the communication to prove their cheating spouse is in fact cheating or attempting to cheat.

Cheating spouses will also sometimes log their IM communication with their lovers. In a few cases, I found logs where the cheater was telling another person that they were not married and they were engaging in highly sexual conversations. In one employment case that I was involved in, a director of operations was using his work computer and logging his IM communication discussing getting a woman and his wife together. He subsequently lost his $200,000.00-a-year position. If your spouse is involved in these activities, there is an enormous potential to find a tremendous amount of information.

There are many companies that provide IP telephony, which is a technical term for using a telephone over a computer network. However, the company that owns Skype.com has taken it to a new level and provides a great service. Anyone can go to www.skype.com, download a free software product, install it on their computer, sign up for a free account, and start talking to anyone anywhere in the world for FREE. The entire process should take less than ten minutes. The software product acts as the phone when it is installed on your computer and all you need to purchase is an Internet headset complete with a microphone. It looks similar to a headset for a cell phone that you may have seen someone wearing while they drive down the road. I have a laptop computer that not only has built-in speakers, but also a built-in microphone. So I did not need to purchase the headset, and I use it all the time to talk to my contacts around the world. It is very simple to use, all your phone calls are not traceable using any phone bill, and you can have conversations from your home, office, and even in your car if you have a broadband wireless access card. Broadband wireless access cards can be purchased from any major wireless provider and enable you to communicate from anywhere there is cell coverage, even while in the middle of a park. Although the free phone service that Skype offers is computer-to-computer and has limitations, it is a great technology that is only going to get better.

In addition to the free phone service using your computer, Skype also offers a variety of paid services that make Skype even more powerful. SkypeOut enables users to make outbound calls to real phone numbers anywhere in the world. It can be a land line or a cell phone; you can now dial that number from your computer. SkypeIn provides the ability to get a real phone number that anyone can call and have it directed to your computer no matter where you are sitting. SkypeVoicemail enables you to set up a voicemail so callers can leave a message when you are not available. These are legitimate and tremendous services offered for free or for a nominal charge that can be set up and taken down in literally minutes. Can you see how easy it would be for cheating spouses to use these technologies to support and further their illicit activities?

Technologies like Skype provide a tremendous service for many legitimate uses, but a growing number of people involved in cheating on their spouses will often use technologies like these to communicate with their lovers. A person who does this doesn't have to worry about leaving telltale signs on a cell phone or line phone bill. There will be signs on their hard drive, such as account names and even logs, that some of these technologies leave there. So, knowing if your spouse has a similar product on their hard drive is important.

There are also many portals that provide a host of other services such as search engines, phone listings, low-cost and even free websites and blogs, as well as other sites that can be used to support and further a cheating spouse's false online identity. Don't assume that just because you find or read about something on the Internet that it is true. For example, suppose you perform a search on a person's name that you want to check out using one of your favorite search engines. The results of your search provide you with three links that show they really work for the company that they said they work for and other links show them involved in other activities that they told you about.

Is there a possibility that some or all of the information that you just found about the individual in a major search engine is false? Absolutely! Search engines get their data in a number of ways. For example, people can make submissions to them directly. Also, they have computer programs that are typically referred to as spiders. These spiders visit each Web page, collect data from each page, and then follow the hyperlinks on each page to other pages, collecting even more data. All of this data is indexed and stored in major databases belonging to the search engine. The process of collecting information has nothing to do with verifying if the information collected is true. If there is information on a Web page, Web forum, or anything Web-based, the search engine spiders will find it and store it. So, if an individual wants you and others to find information about them that may or may not be true, all they have to do is place it on a website, Web forum, blog, or any other type of Web-based application, and the search engines will find, index, and store the information for anyone to find using a search term in their search engine. There is absolutely no way for a search engine to automate the process of verifying the information contained on any Web page. The point is, *Don't believe everything you read.*

I am not saying that everything on the Internet is false; but I am saying that you need to evaluate what you read based on where you are reading it. If you are reading it on the site of a major newspaper or publishing giant, then there is a higher degree of probability that it is true. Only you will be in a position to know if what you are reading is true, so proceed with caution.

I am going to leave you here to absorb the information that I provided in this chapter. I covered a lot of ground and a lot of technology. However, I don't want you to become anxious thinking that your spouse is involved to the point where they are doing *everything* that I covered. The topics that I discussed came from all of my cases and I never had one case where one individual was using all of these technologies to deceive their spouse. I covered the different technologies so you know what is possible and what to look for when you see certain programs on the computer that your spouse uses. I also covered all of these because I am trying to provide enough information to address the needs of all readers, not just those in one specific situation. I encourage you to go on to as many sites as possible to learn what they do and how they do it. As you are reviewing these sites, make a mental note of the site's focus, graphic images, text content, and anything else you can. It may come in handy as you review a computer to see what exactly your spouse is up to. When you start to see certain images and content, you will instantly know what they mean and it will start to paint a picture of your spouse's online activities.

One word of caution: *Never ever use your work computer to review these sites, as in most companies it is a clear violation of policy that might lead to your termination.* Even if you are the only one at work, don't do it. Most companies use monitoring software that will detect and automatically report what each computer is doing or has done on the network. Don't do it! Also, never ever review these sites using the computer that you plan to analyze. You will be the one placing all the images on the computer – and not your spouse – and that might lead you to falsely accuse your spouse. So please make sure you understand technology and how it works before confronting your spouse. Always consult with an attorney before taking such an important step.

– 4 –

Technology Overview

There is very little we do today that does not involve computer technology in some way, shape, or form. Whether we are fueling up at the gas station, paying a highway toll, checking out a book from the library, or purchasing products from our favorite store, technology supports almost every area of our lives. Yet, very few people understand the technology that they use every day.

While most Americans have computers in their homes, there is very little they know about the technology involved and how it could affect them. In the early 1990s, I was quoted in the media: "We lock our doors, we set our alarms, and we think we've locked the world outside. We place a modem in our computer, and we let our children play with criminals." Since the 1990s, an enormous number of cases have been brought against pedophiles in the U.S. for abducting or abusing children they met online. It was what we did not know about technology that subsequently came to hurt us or a member of our family.

Technology has evolved over the past few years, and today there is so much more you need to know about the subject than ever before, especially if you want to learn about recovering data, as well as protecting your identity and privacy. This chapter is designed to introduce you to the various aspects of computer technology that you see every day but take for granted. It is the simple task of turning on a computer to surf online. While technology may seem insignificant, it is important to you for many reasons, especially when it comes to protecting the information that you want to recover. Learning the information is important, so you will need to begin by learning the correct terminology. This will provide you with a tremendous amount of credability, especially when confronting your spouse.

This chapter is not a course on computers in general, but rather it is focused on the basics you need to know in order to locate, recover, and understand the data in a computer. This chapter will not show you *how* to recover the data, but if you lack the technical knowledge that you will read about in this chapter, you will not be able to successfully recover data at all. It is not complicated and I am sure that you will be able to easily grasp and understand the information. Take the time to read and review the information, and do the tasks on a friend's computer, but *never practice on a computer that you wish to recover data from or you may start changing, deleting, and even permanently overwriting data you want to recover.*

There is a difference between computer forensics and data recovery, and I will cover this in greater detail later in the chapter. For now, it is enough to know that the *computer forensic process will enable you to preserve the entire contents of the media as original and will ensure that data is not accidentally modified.* The entire contents means that you not only preserve what is located in the file system, but also what is located in the unallocated or deleted areas of the hard drive. I say media because you can perform computer forensics on a hard drive, USB drive, DVD, or just about any device that stores data – including the small media that fit into cameras. You will only need to perform computer forensics for specific objectives, which will be discussed later.

Data recovery is often referred to when data has been deleted or when a hard drive crashes and you cannot access the drive. For the purpose of this discussion, however, data recovery means locating and accessing specific data, still identified as part of the Windows file system, that you need to analyze. This could be files that contain e-mail and their attachments, Web cache, picture files, or simply Microsoft Word documents.

The most important reasons to understand computer technology are not only to prevent the accidental overwriting and destruction of the data you are attempting to recover, but also to know where the data is stored and how to locate and analyze it. In order to do this, you need to understand how the operating system and file system function, so you know where to find specific data you are looking for, and to understand how and why deleted files can be "unerased." I will take the complex and turn it into easy-to-understand concepts, but it is going to be up to you to read and review the information so that you can understand and retain it. It's not hard, yet it's going to take a little time and effort on your part. It will be well worth it to you in the end. I can tell you that your level of success will be proportionate to the level of effort you expend in learning this information. You can do this, so let's get started.

Computers

A computer in the most basic form is a collection of input and output devices. It is the operating system that is responsible for managing the flow of communication among all of the devices. A monitor is an output device, although it can be an input device if it is a touch monitor like the monitors you see in restaurants where servers enter orders. A mouse is an input device, a keyboard is an input device, and a hard drive is an input/output device (which means that we send data to a hard drive and retrieve data from a hard drive).

Computers come in all shapes and sizes; and for the limited purposes of this book, they can be configured as a desktop or laptop computer. A desktop computer is comprised of numerous components and peripherals. A peripheral is a device that is attached to a computer. Can you name two peripherals? That's right, a mouse and a printer. How about a keyboard? Yes, it is a computer peripheral. See it's not hard; it's the words you never heard before that make it seem more difficult than it really is.

A basic desktop computer has a CPU (Central Processing Unit) housing, a monitor, a mouse, and a keyboard. There also may be speakers, printers, and any number of peripherals attached to the computer. The CPU housing is the main part of the computer, where all the computer components such as the motherboard, processor, hard drive, memory, CD-/DVD-ROM, and other devices that may have been configured when the system was created, are located. In simpler terms, it is the big part of the computer that has the **ON** switch. If you want to learn more about these components, then I encourage you to do so – but they will be outside the scope of this book. The more you know, the more successful you will be.

A basic laptop computer has the same components as a desktop, except the components are all built into one compact housing where the monitor, keyboard, and mouse are located. You can always add an external monitor, mouse, and keyboard to a laptop and use it as though it was a desktop. Manufacturers made this possible because some people like the convenience of a laptop, but can never get used to the pointer mouse, working on a small keyboard, or even working with a smaller monitor. This way, they can use the computer as a laptop while traveling and then use it as a desktop when they are in their office. Who said you can't have two for the price of one?

While it is important to understand the computer and what is attached to it, for the purposes of this book and attaining your objectives, the most important part of that computer is the hard drive. This is the component inside the computer that contains all of the information you are looking to review. You should also be aware that there are external hard drives, USB drives, and CD/DVDs that may contain crucial information. The easiest way to image your spouse's hard drive for a non-technical person will be to use your spouse's computer to create the image, which will be explained later in the book in more detail. Please remember, though, *Never copy or install anything to their hard drive.*

I am covering this information for a reason and I encourage you to start using the correct terminology as it relates to computers and their components or peripherals. The more educated you sound, the more seriously you will be taken. Now you know what a computer is and what components and peripherals can be connected to it. Let's start with what you do every day – when you turn on your computer.

Computer Boot Process

When you depress the **Power** button of the computer to turn the computer **ON**, it goes through a series of checks known as a POST (Power-On Self-Test). This is why you see lights blinking and you can hear the computer beeping. The Power-On Self Test is checking to see what computer components are attached to the computer and that they are functioning properly. One of the first things it does is check the BIOS (Basic Input/Output System) and then the CMOS (Complementary Metal Oxide Semiconductor).

Don't let these terms intimidate you. The BIOS is a chipset located inside your computer that stores instructions for the computer. That's all you need to know about the BIOS. CMOS is pronounced SEE-moss. It apparently was named by someone – probably a computer geek – who did not possess a creative ability for naming computer components, and therefore named it by what it was composed of rather then what it was designed to do. Now that wasn't hard, was it?

The CMOS stores the configuration of the computer, as well as the system date and time. The CMOS is an important feature, so you need to know a little more about it. It is really not that complicated, but there are a few things you might need to know if you have to change the configuration of your system in order to perform computer forensics. Don't get worried that you will have problems doing this because you are not a computer geek. I will walk you through the steps to find the information you are looking for and show you how to change the configuration *only* if it is necessary.

The only change that may be necessary is modifying the computer's boot sequence. Now, even if you don't do that right, you will not harm your computer or cause it to malfunction as long as you don't change anything else while you are in the CMOS. Relax, it's not as complex as you are probably making it out to be. There is an emergency escape from anything you do in the CMOS. If you are unsure of what you may have accidentally changed, then this escape mechanism gives you the option to exit the CMOS without saving the new configuration. Once you do that, the current configuration will be restored and you can then start over.

Now let's say that you cannot find the option to **Exit without saving configuration.** Just shut off the computer. If you cannot find the **OFF** switch, then pull the plug out from the wall. This will not harm your computer, as the configuration is not saved until you choose the option to **Save** it. Also, it will not hurt your computer, since the operating system was not loaded at this point in the boot process. Remember, I am writing this book to help you get through this process, and my goal is to get you through it with the least possible mistakes and the best results. Even the pros make mistakes, so don't worry.

You have seen your computer boot many times, I am sure. You might hear a few tones and see lights illuminate. These lights may be located on a CD-ROM drive. Then, depending on how your computer is configured, you are prompted for your USERNAME AND PASSWORD, or you are brought directly to the desktop of your computer and you can see all the icons on the computer screen. It is also during this boot sequence that the computer will find new devices that have been attached to it since the last time it booted. If it does, it will walk you through the installation of the new device. This is typically referred to as Plug-and-Play Technology. In the past, a computer user had to install driver software so the computer could recognize the new device. Now the computer can tell when you have attached a new device. It will recognize the new device either during the boot process or while the computer is already up and running. The operating system will then install the driver software, if it has it, and will prompt you for a disk if it does not have it.

If you noticed the CD-ROM light illuminate, it is because the CMOS may be configured so the computer will boot to this device, as well as the hard drive. If your computer is looking to boot to your CD-ROM first, this is good, and you should not have to make any changes later if you want to image the drive. This is what is commonly referred to as the boot sequence, so don't be intimidated by it. With one small explanation, you will see how easy it is. The computer is simply looking for an operating system drive to boot and load the operating system. So the boot sequence may be set for CD-ROM drive first, and then hard drive. This means that the computer will first look for an operating system using the CD-ROM drive, and finally the hard drive.

If the computer finds a bootable disk in the CD-ROM, it will load the operating system from that media and you will see a Windows prompt on your screen. If no bootable disk is found in the CD-ROM drive, then the computer will boot to the hard drive, as long as it is working correctly. A bootable disk is a disk that has operating system files installed on it so the computer can recognize it as a bootable disk and it can then load the operating system files from that disk. That's all. *This is important to remember because now you know how to stop the computer from booting to the hard drive, which you may need to do when performing computer forensics.* Booting to the hard drive loads the operating system and uses the system configuration to restrict users based on their security level. Don't let this intimidate you. This is only an issue if your spouse has assigned you a reduced security level and restricted your access. In my experience, this has not been the case, although later in the book you will learn how easy it will be to bypass that security if you need to.

Please remember that you are bound by the law within your jurisdiction, so *do not attempt to access a computer that you are not legally authorized to access.* Booting to the hard drive can also change some file dates and times. While you would like to prevent this any time you can, your spouse does more harm each day they continue to use it, so what you might do by accidentally booting to the hard drive really doesn't matter much. You will not be held to a high standard because you are not a professional who is an expert in computer forensics and data recovery. Your focus is only to get as much data as possible in order to help you make an assessment as to whether or not your spouse is cheating on you. The best characteristics to have in order to perform this are honesty and a strong sense of determination.

In older machines, the default boot sequence was the floppy drive, then the CD-ROM, and then hard drive. If the computer found an operating system diskette in the floppy drive, it would boot to that drive. If it found an operating system bootable CD-ROM in the CD-ROM drive, it would boot to that drive; and if the floppy drive and CD-ROM were empty, then it would then go to the hard drive and boot to that media. I have, though, found newer systems where the boot sequence is set to the hard drive first and then the CD-ROM. This would have to be changed in order to get past the system security. Again, if you accidentally boot to the hard drive, don't worry about it. Just properly power down the computer and try again. Remember, you are not an expert and you will not change anything that will matter.

The next logical question is, *Why would we need to boot to a CD-ROM when we have a perfectly good hard drive to boot to?* Well, therein lies the problem. What if the hard drive was not booting? If the hard drive would not boot, then we could not start the computer and try to copy off the data or even fix the problem all together. A computer user would simply boot to a bootable CD-ROM and many times they would be able to access the hard drive and fix the problems. Remember this because *booting to a CD-ROM instead of the computer's hard drive is key in computer forensics.*

Time for a question. I am asking you this question because I want you to start exercising your mind like a computer forensic technician would. I want you to start to develop the expert in you. *If we boot to an external media source (CD-ROM), what do you think we would bypass?* Stop right here and honestly think about it for a minute. Don't be tempted to read the next sentence, or you will be doing yourself a disservice. If you thought about it for a minute and have an idea, or if you could not think of anything, then read the next sentence.

When you boot to an external media source, you bypass all of the restrictions – including the password – *that have been configured into the operating system by the administrator of the system.* Since you did not boot to the hard drive, you are not bound by its restrictions. WOW! Instant access without any password hassle and you now have full access to the media.

Check with Your Lawyer

I want to take a few seconds to point out an important fact that you must know. Just because you have the knowledge to perform computer forensics, does not mean you have the legal right to do so. Performing computer forensics on a device which you own, considered to be a marital asset, or have access to because it is always brought into your home may be fine, but always check with your lawyer to be sure because the law varies from state to state. Never perform computer forensics unless you consult with an attorney or you may end up in legal hot water. I tell you this because I want to make sure that you follow the laws specific to your circumstances and state jurisdiction. If you don't, all of your efforts may be a waste of your time, especially if you not only lose the right to use the information in a court of law, but also because you may have to defend yourself against criminal statutes. If you are performing computer forensics on a computer belonging to a boyfriend or girlfriend, then you may be in violation of the law and subject to criminal prosecution. Remember, although you do not have a right to access the property of another, check with your lawyer because there may be extenuating circumstances which I am not aware of, where your lawyer may advise you that there is no problem. Never assume that you have the legal right; always check with your lawyer. If you do not have an attorney, find one and consult with them.

If the computer is not configured to boot to the CD-ROM first, then depending on your objectives you may need to change that configuration. So let's get back to booting the computer. When the boot process is completing, one of two things will occur. First, you may be taken directly to the computer's **Desktop** (as there was no USERNAME and PASSWORD required), because this is how your system was configured. Second, you will be prompted for a USERNAME and PASSWORD and once you fill in the criteria and hit **ENTER,** it will finish the boot process and leave you at the computer's **Desktop.** Either way, the system is now in control and you will have access to the computer based on the security level you have been assigned.

CMOS Security

I guess this would be a great time to let you in on a potential issue that might initially nix your plans to change the boot sequence and get any access to the hard drive at all. In fact, if your spouse has enabled this annoying little feature, then that computer won't even boot at all. Before I discuss this issue, I will let you know that there is a way around it.

CMOS has a security feature to prevent people from changing the configuration of the machine. There is also a separate password for the BIOS that will require you to enter a password prior to booting the computer. Now I know what you're about to say: *What the hell do I do now?* Good question: What do you do now? I want you to think about it and then proceed to the next paragraph. Don't cheat because you will only be cheating yourself.

I was hoping you would know. Only kidding! Give it one more guess. Anything? Let's think this through together. What is forcing you to enter the password? Right, the computer. So if you get rid of the computer, there will be nothing to ask for a password. That was simple. Now I know what you're about to say: *Get rid of the computer?* Just take out the hard drive and you can place it in a laptop's drive bay or external hard drive case and attach it to another computer to image. Depending on the computer, it may be easy to accomplish – especially if it is a desktop computer. Yes, you would be able do it. Let's hope you don't have to, but I am sure that most readers could do it.

As I mentioned earlier in the book, I had a client whom I talked through removing the hard drive from a family laptop computer. I told her to practice removing it over the next three days when her husband was at work, and she did. She was really excited when she called me to let me know that she could now do it with her eyes closed and she was ready to go to the next stage. The end result was that her euphoria was soon replaced by disappointment when she found what she thought she would find on the computer. Cheer up, though, because almost 100 percent of the time I have found that there has been no CMOS or BIOS password configured on computers.

Changing the Boot Sequence

We discussed the boot sequence earlier in the chapter, for times when you need the computer to boot to an operating system prior to finding it on the hard drive. The problem with booting to the hard drive is that once you do, the operating system enforces compliance to security that has been configured by the administrator of the system. Most likely, this was your spouse, and you now have limited access.

This might be a little tricky for you, but you need to access the CMOS configuration utility that lets you change the configuration of the computer. The only configuration that you need to change is the boot sequence; but before you do, you have to know how to enter the CMOS configuration utility.

1) First, **Reboot** the computer as the CMOS configuration utility can only be accessed during the boot process in most computers. Some have the ability to access via a DOS prompt, but I don't want to confuse you here so we are all going to do it the same way.

    It is important to know what key or key sequence activates the CMOS configuration utility during the boot process. A key sequence is when you depress one or more keyboard keys down at the same time. In most computers, the only key to depress during the early stages of the boot sequence is one of the following **DEL, ESC, F1, F2, F3,** or the **F10** key. In most cases if you watch the boot process, you will notice a message that often shows up on the screen that states, **Press F2 to enter setup.** Watch for these messages as you perform a test boot. It will be at the very beginning of the boot process.

    Every computer manufacturer not only has a different key or key sequence to hit in order to enter the CMOS configuration utility, but also a designated time to hit that key or key sequence. Some say hit the key when you see certain words on the screen and others say hit the key after a certain screen. However, unless you know when that is, it may be difficult to know when to press the correct key sequence.

2) In my computer it is the **DEL** key. So as soon as I start to see that the system is booting, I hit the **DEL** key once. I typically wait three seconds and hit it again. I do this until the CMOS configuration utility starts. This is the method that should work for you. If you see a **Windows login** prompt or you were brought to the **Windows** desktop, you either did not hit the

key when you were supposed to or the key you were hitting was incorrect. Try it again until you figure it out.

While some manufacturers adhere to industry standards that evolved over the years, others seem to want to create their own, just to be different. That's not always a bad thing, but it can be annoying when you can't figure out how to access the CMOS. Some of the other keys that are used in the industry include a key sequence, which is when several keys must be pressed at the same time. These include the **CTRL + ALT + ESC,** the **CTRL + ALT + A,** and the **CTRL + ALT + S.**

3) Once you are in the configuration utility, you may see numerous settings. Just look around until you see **Boot sequence,** or something similar. If you accidentally hit something and you don't know what you changed, then look for the menu option to **Exit without saving.** This option is always available, and you should exit without saving and start all over. There is also an option to **Restore defaults.** Don't choose this option, as it is better to exit without saving because you don't know what the default settings were. The default settings may not be the current configuration.

Once you locate the option, it really does not matter what sequence you set it for as long as the CD-ROM boots before the hard drive. The changes are accomplished a number of ways, but depend on the manufacturer of the computer. Some use the **PgUp** and **PgDn** keys, while others use the **(+)** and **(–)** keys. Modify the boot sequence, making sure that the CD-ROM boots prior to the hard drive.

Let's say you can't figure it out and you are having a hard time. How would you get that CD-ROM to boot first? Think for a few minutes and then proceed. The best way is to call up your local computer store and ask them to change it for you. It should only cost a nominal fee, but make sure you check the price before you go there. It should take the stress and pressure off you, and you know it will be done right so you can move forward with your plan. All you should have to tell the people at the computer store is that you want the CD-ROM to boot first. While they should not ask you why you want it changed, in case they do and you don't know what to tell them, just say that your spouse purchased a new virus program that requires you to boot to a CD in order to check the entire computer. You could also tell them that it is none of their business; but it is always better to avoid confrontation with people who find it necessary to probe into the affairs of others. It often makes them more curious and more annoying.

It should only take a computer technician about ten minutes to change the boot sequence, but it may take them a little longer if the computer requires a weird key sequence to enter the CMOS. The point is, you should be able to wait for it to be done and should not have to leave your computer. Don't leave it overnight though, or your spouse will suspect something. Make sure you find out when you call the computer store if they can do this while you wait. If they can't, then go someplace else. You might need to tell them the make and model of the computer over the phone before you bring it in, so make sure you have that available when you call.

Windows Security

When you login to your desktop computer and it is not on a domain-controlled network, it is referred to as logging in *locally*. All users are restricted based on their security level that has been assigned to them by the administrator of the computer. The administrator can be any account name as long as that account has administrative privileges. Depending on the version of Windows you are using, accounts can be assigned the following security levels: administrator, power user, user, or guest. Accounts that do not have administrative privileges are limited in what they can do and see.

If you are a user of the computer and do not have administrative privileges, then you will most likely not be able to access areas of the file system that you need to access. Don't worry, because later in the book I will show you how to easily get past all that. It would, though, be nice to know if your spouse has restricted your access. There are two ways to determine this. The first is by viewing the **User accounts** listing.

1) To access this information, bring your pointer to the **Start** icon located at the bottom left of the computer screen and **Left-Click** the mouse, which will bring up a menu. (You can also accomplish this by just hitting the **WINDOWS** key on your keyboard. This is the key that has the Windows logo on it.)

2) Look for and then bring your mouse up to highlight the menu item **Settings,** which will bring up another menu.

3) Look for and then **Double-click** on the menu item **Control panel.** This will open another window, which is your computer's **Control panel.** (You can also accomplish this by holding down the **WINDOWS** key and the **E** key at the same time, which will open a Windows Explorer™ window. You will then notice on the left side of the screen the option, **Control panel.** Just **Click** on this option once, and it will open the **Control panel.)**

4) Toward the bottom of the icon listings, you will notice an icon of a man and a woman which is titled **User accounts. Double-click** this icon and you will see a list of **User accounts.**

5) The account name is the name you use to login to the computer. So if you login to the computer using JANE, then your account will be named JANE. If you see only your account name, then your access is limited. If you see an account titled ADMINISTRATOR, then you have administrative access. (While the ADMINISTRATOR account can be disabled, it cannot be deleted, since it is a default system account.)

The second way to determine if you have full access is through the Windows file system.

1) In order to access the file system, bring your pointer to the **Start** button again, and this time **Right-click** the mouse once, which will bring up a menu.

2) Toward the top of the menu you will see the **Explore** option.

Left-click once on the **Explore** option and it will open up a split window.

3) The left side of the window is slimmer and you can view the file structure in it. The right window displays the contents of any folder that is highlighted on the left side. (As an alternative to **Left-clicking** on the **Explore** option, you can also accomplish this by holding down the **WINDOWS** key and depressing the **E** key at the same time.)

4) Toward the top of the left window, you will see some words or numbers followed by **(C:).** This is your system hard drive and it is the first physical drive your computer found, which is why it is given the **(C:)** designation. The words or numbers just to the left of the **(C:)** is the label the drive was given. This label can be changed and might have been assigned by the manufacturer or by your spouse.

5) Down below the line that has **(C:),** you will notice a folder that is named DOCUMENTS AND SETTINGS. If you don't see the listing below that line, this means that there should be a **(+)** sign just to the left of the **(C:).** If this is the case, then **Click** on that **(+)** sign and it will turn into a **(–)** sign and the listing will appear. The **(+)** sign means that the folder has other subfolders and/or files inside it and has not been expanded to view the listing. Hitting the **(+)** sign expands the listing and hitting the **(–)** sign collapses the listing. If there is no plus or minus sign, then the folder has no subfolders in it.

6) **Click** on the DOCUMENTS AND SETTINGS folder once and it will show you the contents of that folder in the right window pane. Even if you have limited access, you will still be able to see the ADMINISTRATOR PROFILE folder. However, if you attempt to access the ADMINISTRATOR PROFILE folder, you will receive an error stating that you do not have permission. If you **Click** on the ADMINISTRATOR PROFILE folder and do not get an error, then you have Administrative access. All the accounts on the system will be in this folder and every folder

name is typically an account on the system except for two folders, which are ALL USERS and DEFAULT USER folders. So if you see a folder named ROBERT in the DOCUMENTS AND SETTINGS folder, then ROBERT is a USERNAME that is used to login to the computer system. Now you know what level you have been assigned.

Gaining Administrative Access

This section again assumes that you have the legal right to access the entire computer and that you are correct in your assessment that you do not have *administrative access* to the computer. If you are in doubt about your security level assignment, please refer to the prior section in this chapter titled "Windows Security," which will take you through the process of making that determination. I want you to be sure, because there is no sense in purchasing a product and taking additional steps to bypass something you don't need to bypass.

In order to bypass the security on a computer, you need to purchase a software application that will modify your security level or toggle the password off for the current administrative user account. While there are many applications on the market that you can find using an Internet search, for the purposes of this chapter we will be focusing on the FTK™ Imager product published by the Access Data Corporation. Additional information about the company and its products can be found at www.AccessData.com. *(See also page 106.)*

Please understand that this CD also is intended for use by professionals in the industry who are experts in technology and need access to powerful application features. Since you are not an expert, I am going to ask you not to use certain options provided on this CD. For example, **Option 3** is titled **Change login password.** This will give you the ability to change a user's password.

You need to be aware that if you change a user's password and they have EFS (Encrypted File System) implemented on their computer, then they may never get access to that data again. *Please stay out of Option 3 and any other option unless you are sure you know what you are doing.*

This option will enable you to backup the SAM and SYSTEM file, but you must know what you are doing to be successful. *Don't take the chance if you are not an expert.*

1) The first step is to **turn the computer OFF.**

2) Then place the bootable CD that you received from the Access Data Corporation in the CD-ROM drive and **Power on** the computer. The computer will then go through the normal boot process.

   If you are brought to a **Windows** login prompt or if you are brought to the computer **Desktop,** then the boot sequence was not set the way you need it to be. If this was the case, then it is apparent that the computer did not look to the CD-ROM drive first during the boot sequence. Please go back to the prior section in this chapter titled "Changing the Boot Sequence" and follow the directions carefully to make sure the computer boots the way you need it to.

3) If the boot sequence was set correctly, then you will be brought to a screen that is titled **Access Data FTK Imager** and **XPAccess,** which is centered at the top of the screen. The screen will have three menu options, which include **Image a hard drive, Modify login access** and **Change login password.** Don't be alarmed by the name XPAccess, as this product is intended for use on most Windows platforms, including Windows 2000 and Windows XP.

4) Choose **Option 2, Modify login access.** *Please do not choose Option 3 at all.* Highlight **Option 2** using the **ARROW** keys and then hit **ENTER** or the **SPACE BAR.**

5) Once you do this, you will be brought to another screen that will have two options, which are **Modify user rights** and **Toggle on/off login password.**

I think that it is important for you to understand both options in order to choose one. They will both accomplish the same result in the end, but there are reasons that you may choose one over the other.

The first option allows you to actually change the user rights of user accounts on the computer. So if you personally had an account on the computer system, but had limited rights, then this option would allow you to increase your user rights to administrative rights on the system and you would then have full access to the system. Remember, you need *administrative rights* to image the entire hard drive if you want to do this the easy way by using your spouse's computer.

You might want to choose this option if you had an account on the computer so no one could accuse you of using another user's login name to access a computer. This may be an issue in some states but not others, so you must check with your lawyer before making this decision. He or she would be in the best position to guide you to the correct way legally. The decision to choose which option is based on semantics and legal positioning, but has no technical bearing whatsoever, as both will help you accomplish what you need to accomplish – obtaining administrative rights on the system.

Lawyers should realize, however, that there is a difference between the user account JSMITH and the user account ADMINISTRATOR. While only your spouse may be JSMITH, why should you be precluded from accessing the computer as administrator? What makes your spouse the administrator and not you? The answer is nothing, and lawyers should realize that from a technical point of view.

The ADMINISTRATOR account is a default user account that was created by the Microsoft Corporation, not your spouse. The nice feature about this account is that it can never be deleted and it will always be there for you to modify the access rights. So even if your spouse has disabled the account, you can re-enable that account. It is no more your spouse's account than it is your account. You should have the equal right to access that account or have the legal ability to change the rights on that account if they have that right. What makes your spouse in charge of the computer? The answer is absolutely nothing.

While I am not an attorney nor a judge, I cannot think of any legal reason that would say that one spouse controls the issuance of all rights and privileges and decides who gets what access rights to a marital asset. I am mentioning this because I believe it may be important to discuss this topic with your lawyer, and I want to make sure you have the technical information to supply them with so they have the ammunition to fight for your rights.

The second option allows you to select a user and toggle off their password. This means when you login to the computer and you are prompted for a USERNAME AND PASSWORD, all you have to do is enter the USERNAME, leaving the PASSWORD blank, and then hit the **ENTER** key. The computer will log you in using that USERNAME *without* their PASSWORD. This would be another option you could choose if you personally have *no* account on the computer and the one and only *user account* on the computer was being used by your spouse. Read that last sentence again so you can see exactly what I said there. Notice that I *did not* say that the only existing account belonged to your spouse. This is because if there is only one account, that would be the ADMINISTRATOR account. Again I ask: *What makes it their account and not yours if it is a default Microsoft user account?* – nothing!

I will now walk you through the process of modifying user rights and toggling off and on a user's password.

1) Let's start with **Option 1, Modifying user rights.** I am assuming that you have already booted to the CD and from the **Main menu** you chose **Modify login access.**

2) The two options on the screen should be **Modify user rights** and **Toggle off/on user password.** Please choose **Option 1** using the **ARROW** keys, and either hit the **ENTER** key or the **SPACE BAR.**

3) This will bring you to another screen that lists all the users of the system. The USERNAMES will be listed with either admin rights or limited rights written just to the right of the USERNAME.

4) Choose your account by using the **ARROW** keys and then hit the **ENTER** key or **SPACE BAR,** and it will change the current access rights.

5) Once you see the **Access rights change**, hit the **ESC** key and you will be prompted to **Save** the new configuration.

6) Once you are prompted, just hit the **Y** key, and it will bring you back to the previous menu.

7) Then hit the **ESC** key again, and it will bring you back to the **Main menu.**

8) Then hit the **ESC** key one more time, and the application will ask if you want to **Reboot** the computer.

9) Then hit the **Y** key and the computer will **Reboot.**

   Please take the CD out of the CD drive or the computer will boot to the CD again.

10) Let the computer boot to the **Login** prompt, and then **Login** to the computer using your own login account and you will be ready to image the hard drive.

11) When you are done imaging the drive, you must go through the process again and **Reduce your access rights.** If you don't and your spouse notices that you have administrative rights, that will make them very suspicious. Remember, you can change your access rights any time you want, so just change it back for now or you may lose the opportunity to image the hard drive again in the future.

    This is an important part of the process so please make sure to complete it. You want to retain the element of surprise.

Now let's assume that you do not have an account on the computer system and your lawyer has advised you that you *do* have a legal right to image the hard drive.

1) Then choose **Option 2** from the **Modify login access** menu. Once you choose **Option 2,** you will again get a list of all the users on the system with their respective security levels. However, you will also notice the words **Password on** or **Password off** just to the right of their security level.

2) Highlight the USERNAME you want to toggle off their password using the **ARROW** keys and then hit the **ENTER** key or **SPACE BAR.**

3) This will change the wording **Password on** to **Password off.**

4) Then hit the **ESC** key and it will prompt you to **Save** the new configuration.

5) Hit the **Y** key when prompted with this message, and it will take you back to the previous menu.

6) Then hit the **ESC** key again and it will take you back to the **Main menu.**

7) Then hit the **ESC** key again and the application will ask if you want to **Reboot** the computer.

8) Hit the **Y** key and the computer will start the reboot process.

   Please make sure to take the CD out of the CD drive or it will boot to the CD again.

9) When the computer **Reboots,** it will take you to the **Login** prompt.

10) Enter the USERNAME of the account, leaving the PASSWORD blank and hit the **ENTER** key. This will log you into the computer and you will have the full rights of that user. You should now be ready to image the hard drive.

11) When you are done imaging the drive, you must go through the process again and **Toggle back on their password.** If you don't and your spouse notices that they no longer need a PASSWORD to login, that will make them very suspicious. Remember, you can change it any time you want so just change it back for now or you may lose to opportunity to image the hard drive again in the future. *This is an important part of the process so please make sure to complete it.* You want to retain the element of surprise.

Now let's get acquainted with the **Desktop.**

Windows Desktop

The picture you see on the Windows desktop is referred to as the desktop background. This can be easily changed, but it is outside the scope of this book. The icons on the desktop are typically shortcuts to start applications that have been installed on the computer. An icon can also be a shortcut to a document or folder containing documents. An icon is a small graphic or picture. If you know a lot of this already, don't worry as there will be more complex things coming very shortly that will certainly challenge your mind. Besides, reviewing the information will help reinforce what you already know. I must review the basics in order to make sure I address the needs of the readers who are not as familiar with computers as you might be. So please bear with me.

If you look to the bottom left side of the screen, you will see an icon titled **Start.** This is referred to as the **Start** icon, which is used for several tasks, some of which you have already used in prior sections of this book. Just to the right of the **Start** icon is a gray bar that hugs the bottom of the screen and stretches from the left side of the screen all the way to the right side of the screen. This is referred to as the **Taskbar.** Sometimes the system is configured with an auto-hide **Taskbar** feature. You will know this when you login and do not see the **Taskbar** at the bottom of the screen. When you place the pointer down by the **Taskbar** area, however, it magically appears. Since Windows is designed to be configured based on each user, the **Taskbar** can be easily moved and it can be located along the right side of the screen or the left. Why people do this is up to them, but I just want to point this out to you in case you see the **Taskbar** some place other than where I said it would be.

Depending on how you may have installed applications, you may see a set of icons on the left side of the **Taskbar** close to the **Start** icon and another set of icons on the right side of the **Taskbar.** The icons on the left side are **Quick start** icons for applications. They need to be **Clicked** only once and the application they are associated with will start. You can simply drag an icon from the **Desktop** to the **Quick start** portion of the **Taskbar** and it will be added to the **Quick start** list.

The icons on the right side of the **Taskbar** are applications and process that have been loaded into the computer's memory and are either running processes or inactive. There is a configuration that allows users to hide the inactive process icons, but these can be quickly viewed with the **Click** of the (**<**) icon. Remember, this is just so you know this information, even though it may not be relevant to computer forensics. Don't get overwhelmed and just take it slow. You will become more familiar with computers and soon people will listen to you speak and see the expert in you.

System Date and Time

An important part of computer forensic process is validating the current system date and time by checking the settings located in the CMOS. However, I would rather that you validate the computer's date and time by using the **Control panel** in order to avoid any issues. This is important, especially if the dates and times of the files are crucial. It does you no good to protect the file dates and times if you don't even know if the system date and time are correct. How could you authenticate the actual date and time of the files if you don't know if the computer's internal clock is correct? Remember, it was the computer's internal clock that the computer used to stamp the file dates and times.

I have had cases where the dates have been off by hours, days, months, and even years. A review of my cases over many years would reveal that in about 65 percent of my cases the system time has been off between 0 and 10 minutes; in 15 percent of my cases, the system time has been off by hours; and in 5 percent of my cases, the system date has been off by days. I have had one or two cases where the system date has been off by months and even years, but was most likely due to a dead CMOS battery. The CMOS battery is what keeps the internal clock active when the computer is unplugged. The battery will literally last for years, but it can even be worn down to nothing. However, due to the rate at which people have been changing their computers to keep up with technology, the possibility of killing a CMOS battery is almost zero.

Let's now learn how to check the system date and time of the computer.

1) Take your pointer down to the **Start** button again and **Left-click** once. This will bring up a menu.

2) Move your pointer up the menu and highlight the **Settings** option, which will bring up another menu.

3) Highlight the **Control panel** option and **Left-click** once. This will open the **Control panel** window.

   You can also accomplish this by holding down the **WINDOWS** key and the **E** key at the same time. This will open a Windows Explorer window. In the left pane of the Windows Explorer window you will see an option titled **Control panel. Click** on this option once, and it will open the **Control panel.**

4) Toward the top of the icon listing you will notice the words **Date and time,** as well as an icon of a clock and calendar.

5) **Click** on the words or the icon and it will open the **Date and time** properties.

Make sure to record the system date and time and compare it to another verifiably accurate source. Can you think of a source that might be proved to be accurate? Yes, your cell phone provider. Note the date and time of the computer and then note the date and time on your cell phone. Then figure out if the computer is set to the exact time or how fast or slow the computer time may have been set. Also note the current time zone the computer is set for. Remember, if the time is off, it may be that the computer was set like that accidentally or purposely. It does not have to mean that the computer's clock is no longer accurate.

There is a lot of other technical information that would be useful to know but *that* exceeds the scope of this book. The goal of this book is to bring you up to speed as quickly as possible with the minimum amount of information so you can get off to a good start. You may not need a lot of this information to find and analyze the data, but you need it to understand why you can and that is important. So I will leave you here and look forward to seeing you at the next chapter.

5

Windows File System

N ow it is time to discuss the Windows file system and how we can navigate it. This is very important for you to learn because you must know how files are created and stored, as well as how to navigate the Windows file system to locate specific data. This is the way you will find Internet cache and E-mail files that contain all of your spouse's e-mail. These files can then be copied to another computer and searched, reviewed, and printed by using simple utilities that we will discuss later in the chapter covering e-mail. It is not hard, and I will soon have you navigating the Windows file system like a pro and best of all, you will gain a greater understanding of Windows technology.

I don't want you to become overwhelmed by the amount of words, pages, or tasks that I am teaching you in this chapter. If we sat down together, I have no doubt that you could learn everything in this chapter in about ten minutes. It is that easy! It just looks like a lot to learn, but it's not. The best way to attack this chapter is to learn one task, then practice it, and then move on. It will go quicker that way and you will absorb and comprehend more. Remember, the more you practice the better you will become.

I also want you to understand that this is not a Windows course. The purpose of this chapter is to give you enough information to obtain what you need and then take your time to analyze the information. A lot of information about the Windows file system and shortcuts to navigate the system will not be covered. I have chosen the tools you need to accomplish your objectives and these are the ones you need to focus on. I do, however, encourage you to learn more by either taking a course or reading a book that specifically deals with the ins and outs of the Windows file system.

Windows is comprised of an operating system and a file system that makes it easy for us to interact with the computer. The operating system controls the flow of information among devices and peripherals, as we discussed in the last chapter. The file system stores and manages application and system files, as well as files created by the end-user. These files are organized using the concept of folders. You can think of these folders as filing drawers. You open one drawer for letters that you have written to your family members and another draw for letters to your clients. It is the same way you organize your paper files.

Understanding Files and Folders

Almost everyone creates files on their hard drive, either directly or indirectly. Do you know that when you surf the Web, you are creating files on your hard drive? No, not you directly, but your actions of surfing the Web causes files to be cached on your hard drive.

You also create files when you make word-processing documents, spreadsheets, and graphic files, for example. Your data is stored in a specific file type based on its data contents. For example, Microsoft Word documents are stored in Microsoft word format and have a file extension of .DOC, Star Office documents by Sun Micro Systems have a file extension of .SXW, and graphic files are stored in many formats which include file extensions of .JPG, .TIF, and .BMP. (File extensions are the letters following the period (.) at the very end of the file name. Example: for LETTER.DOC, the file extension is .DOC.)

Video clips are stored with file extensions of .MPG, .MOV, and .WMV. These file extensions are just some of the literally thousands of file data formats. Files are also created on your hard drive when you install applications, and file dates and times are also modified when you uninstall applications. You can see how many ways data is created on your hard drive and this happens every time you use your computer.

The Windows file system organizes its electronic files the same way. Most applications that are installed are placed in a folder called PROGRAM FILES. Then, inside that folder (or filing drawer) there is another folder that bears the title of the application. If you just looked into the PROGRAM FILES folder, you would most likely see other folders named MICROSOFT OFFICE™, QUICKBOOKS™, QUICKTIME™, and AMERICA ONLINE™, just to name a few. In a perfect world if you looked into your PROGRAM FILES folder, you would see all the programs that are currently installed on your computer.

There may be some exceptions to that rule and it all depends on the company that created the application. While most adhere to a standard of placing their applications in the PROGRAM FILES folder, there are a few that place them right in the root of the hard drive. The root of the hard drive means that it is not placed into any folder or subfolder of the hard drive. If you highlight the hard drive icon, you will see the PROGRAM folder right there, instead of in the PROGRAM FILES folder. You can see that the Microsoft Corporation organizes files into folders and organizes these folders by category into other folders. Microsoft set the standard, but remember it's up to the companies who created the application to follow that standard.

To see this, let's take a look at the file system on your computer.

1) I want you to take your pointer and place it on top of the **Start** icon. Don't click the **Start** icon yet, just let the pointer lie on top of the **Start** icon. The pointer is typically a short arrowhead, but on today's computers, it can be shaped like anything, including a dinosaur. Either way, I'm referring to the pointer that moves around the screen when you move the mouse.

2) Now, please **Right-click** your mouse and you will notice that it brings up a new menu with several options. Look for the menu option titled **Explore,** which should be the second one from the top. (The top menu option is most likely **Open,** and just below that menu option is **Explore.) Click** on **Explore** and you will notice that a new window opens. You also can accom-

plish this by holding down the **WINDOWS** key and hitting the **E** key at the same time. This window may or may not expand to the full size of your screen.

3) Take a look at the very top right of the new window. There you will notice three icons. There will be an **X** all the way to the right of the window. The icon to the left of the **X** should be either a **Single box** or a **Double box,** and the icon to the left of the box will look like a minus sign (–) or hyphen. If you have a **Single box,** then **Click** on the **Single box,** and you will notice that the window fills the screen on your monitor and the icon then changes to a **Double box.**

If it is a **Double box, Click** on it and it will reduce the size of the window and it will then change to a **Single box.**

Click on the **Single box** again, and the window once again fills the screen, and the icon changes again to a **Double box.**

Now **Click** on the icon that looks like a hyphen (–), and the window will seem to disappear. It has not disappeared – it is now minimized. You can also accomplish this by holding down the **WINDOWS** key and depressing the **D** key. That means that this particular window was taken out of your way so you can access your **Desktop** or other applications behind the window. However, if you look at the bottom of the screen, you should see an icon shaped like a rectangle on the **Taskbar**. This icon looks like it is popping out at you. The title of the icon will depend on what was highlighted before you minimized it. If you had the PROGRAM FILES folder high-lighted, the minimized rectangle on the **Taskbar** will say PROGRAM FILES. **Left-click** on the minimized icon on the **Taskbar,** and it will maximize the window again. You can also accomplish this by holding the **WINDOWS** key down and depressing the **D** key again. So you can see that you can mini-mize and maximize any window with the (–) icon, using the **Taskbar** or the **Windows** shortcut keys.

4) Let's make sure the window is maximized and review the open window. The open window is organized with menu options along the top of the screen and most of the window is broken into two window panes. The one on the left is smaller and has **Desktop** on the very top, followed by **MyDocuments, MyComputer,** and other options below that. If you see something a little different, this is most likely because you are using a different version of the Windows operating system, and it also depends on how your computer is configured.

5) You are now looking at the file system of the computer. If you look farther down, you will see a name or series of numbers followed by **(C:).** This is the system hard drive and all the files and folders that it contains are structured in a "tree" below it. If you do not see this file tree structure, then look to the left of the **(C:)** and you will see a **(+)** sign. If you see this **(+)** sign, that means that the file tree structure has been collapsed. In order to expand the file structure tree, just **Click** on the **(+)** sign and the file tree structure will appear just below the **(C:).**

If you take your pointer and **Click** on the **(C:),** you will see several folders show up in the right pane. The left pane displays the drives and the folders contained on each of the drives and the right pane will display the contents of the drives or folders when they are chosen (highlighted) in the left pane.

6) If you highlight the **(C:)** line and **Right-click** once, a menu will appear. The bottom option on this menu should be **Properties.** Navigate your way down to the **Properties** option and you will see another window appear. This will show you the size of the hard drive and show you what percentage of the hard drive has data and what percentage of the hard drive has free space. *This will be crucial information when you are planning to purchase an external USB drive.* You can also highlight any folder on the hard drive and perform the same steps in order to find how much data a certain folder contains. So if you were looking to just copy a PROFILE folder located in the

DOCUMENTS AND SETTINGS folder, you can just highlight it and discover what size hard drive you would need to copy that folder. You may only need a small USB drive to copy that folder.

7) **Scroll up** to the top of the left pane. You can do this by using the **Scrollbar** that separates the left pane from the right pane. It is visible only when the list of folders exceeds below the bottom of the left pane. If there is a very thin gray line between the left and right panes, then the **Scrollbar** is not visible. The **Scrollbar** is much thicker and you will notice that it moves up and down. The folders are depicted by the **Manila Folder** icon and the files are depicted by many different icons. The icons that represent the files are chosen by the company that published the program file.

8) Make sure that the line that has **(C:)** is highlighted. This will display the contents of the **(C:)** drive in the right window pane. Then **Double left-click** on any of the folders located in the right pane and you will see the files and folders located in that folder. These will show up in the right pane. If you look on the **Taskbar,** you will see the name of the folder that is highlighted. This is basically a visual reminder on the **Taskbar** of what folder you are currently in.

Now look in the left window pane again, but this time toward the very bottom. If you have a CD-ROM or DVD in the computer, this might show up as **(D:).** If you have an external USB drive attached to the computer, then that might show up as **(E:).** If you do not have a CD-ROM or DVD, but you do have a USB drive attached to the computer, it would be the **(D:)** drive. Windows assigns drives attached to the computer in sequence. You should, however, be able to distinguish the CD-ROM or DVD drive from the USB drive because Windows will also place a small icon of a **CD** next to the drive. This should be a tip-off that this is the CD-ROM or DVD drive. External USB drives often show up labeled as **Local disk**, **Removable Disk** or **Public,** which is sometimes based on how the manufacturer labeled the drive.

9) Before you leave this section, I want to teach you how to create a folder on the local hard drive of your friend's computer. This is very simple and you can delete it when you are done. So open Windows Explorer using the **WINDOWS** key and the **E** key at the same time.

10) Now highlight the **(C:)** drive in the left window pane. When you do that, the root of drive **(C:)** will show up in the right window pane.

11) **Right-click** anywhere in the right window pane – just once. This will bring up a small menu and one of the options toward the bottom of the menu should be **New.**

12) Highlight the **New** option and another menu should appear.

13) The option at the top should be **Folder.** I want you to **Click** on the **Folder** option. Now look down at the bottom of the right pane and you will see that a new folder has appeared and it is titled NEW FOLDER.

14) If you just hit the **BACKSPACE** key once the name NEW FOLDER will disappear and you can type any name you want.

15) Then **Left-click** anywhere off that NEW FOLDER, and it will finalize the naming of that folder.

   Sometimes people hit a key by accident and it keeps the name NEW FOLDER. In that case, all you have to do is highlight the folder and then **Right-click** and choose the **Rename** option. You will then be where you should have been, so just hit the **BACKSPACE** key and then type the new name for the folder.

16) If you **Double-click** on the NEW FOLDER, it will take you inside the folder and you will see that it is empty. Wow! You created a folder in the root of the hard drive. If you want to delete it, all you have to do is highlight the folder and then **Right-click** on that folder. A small menu will appear and all you have to do is **Click** on the **Delete** option and it will disappear.

How to Copy Files and Folders

It is important to make sure you understand the prior section in this chapter, as that will make it much easier to comprehend this one. Learning how to navigate your way from folder to folder and drive to drive is important. You should become familiar with all the tasks in the prior section before beginning this section. If you need a little extra time before starting this section, then take that time to learn what you need to.

We are going to dive into a great exercise headfirst. I am going to tell you some very important information right now and we will use this information to conduct an exercise in order to practice copying files from one drive to another. I do want to make it clear that *you should not practice this for the first time on your spouse's computer.* Never start to learn using the target computer because it will only lead to mistakes. The time to make mistakes is when you are learning on a friend's computer, not when you are trying to recover data or perform a drive image on your spouse's computer.

That being said, the most important information that you will be looking for that is still part of the Windows file system is located in the DOCUMENTS AND SETTINGS folder. All the PROFILES are located in the DOCUMENTS AND SETTINGS folder. Copying one of the PROFILE folders and all the subfolders to an external USB drive will give you the ability to take the data offsite to review without interruption and without being discovered by your spouse. The PROFILE folder is the same name as the USERNAME they used to login to the computer. So, if their USERNAME was JSMITH, the PROFILE folder would be JSMITH.

There is one exception to that rule, and it has to do with Windows XP Home Edition. Windows XP Home Edition has a default USER account named OWNER. Even if you change the account name, the PROFILE folder for this account remains OWNER. So remember to be alert when looking through the DOCUMENT AND SETTINGS folder for the OWNER PROFILE folder.

The PROFILE folder contains all of the Web cache, all the e-mail, as well as all pictures and documents for that specific user. Remember, there are a few exceptions depending on the version of Microsoft that you are using and on the e-mail client that your spouse uses and whether or not the publisher of that e-mail software follows the Microsoft standard; most do.

There is one issue that you need to understand before proceeding. If you share the same login USERNAME with your spouse and you in fact login using that account and attempt to copy the PROFILE folder, you will experience a "copying error" as there are system files in use, which you cannot copy while they are in use. One of these files is the NTUSER.DAT file. Instead of just skipping the system files in use, the entire copy process will be aborted by Windows. For example, if you login as JSMITH and then attempt to copy the JSMITH PROFILE folder this will invoke the "copying error" because the PROFILE folder is in use, as you logged in as JSMITH.

So if you are logging in using the same account as your spouse, you have to copy specific folders that do not contain system files that are in use by the account. Then you can go into the folders that have system files and copy only the files you need, avoiding system files such as NTUSER.DAT.

If you login using a different account that has administrative privileges, then you can copy your spouse's PROFILE folder with no problem. If there is no other account, however, please do not add one or you may inadvertently destroy data. (This can all be avoided when you use forensic software to acquire the image of your spouse's computer.)

There is one other issue that has to do with Windows XP Home Edition that you need to be aware of. The Windows XP Home Edition only allows the ADMINISTRATOR account to copy other PROFILE folders. So, if you are not imaging the hard drive and you want to copy your spouse's PROFILE folder, you must login using the ADMINIS-TRATOR account.

Okay, let's get back to learning how to copy folders and files.

Begin by starting Windows Explorer.

1) In order to access Windows Explorer, hold down the **WINDOWS** key and then depress the **E** key at the same time. This will open the Windows Explorer window.

2) **Click** on the **(+)** sign to the left of the **(C:)**, and this will expand the WINDOWS FILE TREE under the **(C:)** drive.

3) **Scroll down** and **Expand** the DOCUMENTS AND SETTINGS folder, which will reveal all the PROFILE folders. A PROFILE folder is named after the user account, so if your friend logs in as administrator, there will be a folder named ADMINIS-TRATOR. If they logged in as ROGER or NANCY, then there will be a folder named either ROGER or NANCY. That is an easy-to-understand concept.

4) **Highlight** the PROFILE folder you want to practice on and then using your mouse, **Right-click.** This will bring up a small menu.

5) I want you to **Scroll down** that menu to the **Copy** option and **Left-click** once on **Copy.** You have just copied that folder, all its subfolders, and all its files into the memory of the computer. This can also be accomplished by hitting a two-key sequence – the **CTRL** key and the **C** key at the same time.

6) Now, **Scroll down** the left window pane until you see your USB drive. It may be labeled **(D:)**. Highlight that **(D:)** drive, and then **Right-click** on it. This will bring up that small menu again.

7) This time, please **Scroll down** and **Click** on **Paste.** This can also be accomplished by hitting a two-key sequence, the **CTRL** button and the **V** key. (They must be depressed at the same time.) You will then see all of the files being copied from the **(C:)** drive to the **(D:)** drive.

8) Now that you have the data on the USB drive, you cannot just simply disconnect that drive from the computer. The USB drive has to be stopped first or you may start to induce corruption to either one of the drive or files on either of the drives.

9) You can stop the USB drive very easily by **Clicking** on a small icon that is located on the right side of the **Taskbar** located at

the bottom of the screen. The icon looks like a flat card with a green **Arrow** over it. When you **Left-click** on that icon once, it will bring up a very small menu which will list the drives attached to the computer.

10) **Click** on the USB drive, and you should receive a message shortly after that it is now safe to remove the drive. It is then safe to remove the cable from the computer.

Now that you have learned how to copy an entire folder of data, copying files is no different. All you do is highlight one or more files and then **Right-click** and then **Left-click** on the **Copy** option. Then **Highlight** the destination drive or folder where you want the files to be copied to and then **Right-click** and then **Left-click** on the **Paste** option and all the files will be copied to that location. So as far as copying goes, there is absolutely no difference between copying files and copying folders.

In order to copy more than one file or folder, all you have to do is **Left-click** on each item that you want to copy while holding down the **CRTL** key. This will highlight all the files and/or folders in a blue color. Once they are all highlighted, just **Right-click** on top of any one of the blue files or folders and then **Left-click** on the **Copy** option. This will copy all of the files and or folders into the memory of the computer. **Highlight** the drive and/or folder you want to copy the files to, then **Right-click,** and then **Left-click** on the **Paste** option. All of the files and/or folders will start to copy to the new destination.

Now that you have completed that exercise, it is time to pretend that you are taking the data off-site for review. Since I truly believe that you did not perform this for the first time on your spouse's computer and you were actually working on a friend's computer, please plug that USB drive back into your friend's computer and let's navigate around to see what we can.

1) Open the Windows Explorer by holding the **WINDOWS** key down while depressing the **E** key.

2) Then navigate your way to the USB drive, which for purposes

of this exercise will be the **(D:)** drive. This may be different for your computer, so please make sure.

3) Let's assume that for the purposes of this exercise the PROFILE folder you copied to the USB drive was named ROGER. Navigate your way to this PROFILE folder and **Double-click** on the folder.

4) Once you open this folder, you should see another folder named LOCAL SETTINGS. **Double-click** on this folder, which will bring you to the file and folder listing in that folder.

5) Look for and **Double-click** on a folder named TEMPORARY INTERNET FILES. This will bring you to a listing of all the Web cache for that user. The Web cache folder will contain both cookies and pictures, which you should be able to view using Windows Explorer. If you only see a listing when you are in the folder, then you must change the view of what you are looking at.

6) This is very important so read this paragraph and the next very carefully. *If you do not see a folder named* LOCAL SETTINGS, *it does not have anything to do with your security level because you should already have administrative access. If you don't have administrative access, then you would not be able to access the* PROFILE *folders. The inability to view* SYSTEM *folders has everything to do with the current view setting identified in the* **Folder options** *configuration panel.*

To change this, you must take your pointer to the top of the screen and **Left-click** on the **Tools** option. This will open a small menu.

7) **Scroll down** to the bottom and **Click** on **Folder options**.

8) Once you do this, you will see three tabs at the top of the panel. I want you to **Click** on the middle tab, which is the **View** tab.

9) A little more than halfway down the initial listing in the panel, you will see a folder icon with the words HIDDEN FILES AND FOLDERS next to it. Just below this there are two options, one being **Do not show hidden files and folders,** and the second being, **Show hidden files and folders.** I want you to make sure to **Click** on the **Second** option.

10) At the top, **Click** on the button **Apply to all folders.**

11) **Click** on the **OK** button at the bottom of the panel and you should be able to see the folders you need. Remember this because you may have to use this again for other folders you may want to access but can't see because of this setting.

12) In order to change the view, take your pointer and move up to the top of the screen, where you will see a menu that runs along the top of the window. One of the options is **View,** which is the third option from the left as you move to the right. **Click** on the **View** option and this will open a menu of view types.

13) **Click** on the **View option for thumbnails,** which will display the pictures. However, other file types may show up as other icons, including small note pads if it is a cookie.

Cookies are small text files that websites use to track your movements at their site. If the PROFILE name was ROGER, then some of the cookies might be named roger@yahoo.com. If you see an icon of a big blue **e,** this is most likely a Windows Internet Explorer icon, which is an .HTML file or, in other words, a Web page. If you **Double-click** on any of the cookies or the .HTML files, you will see a warning about executing an application. They are not applications, so don't worry about it. Choose **Yes,** and you will be able to view the files. It is important to review the cookies, graphic files and Web pages – all of which may reveal what your spouse is doing online.

Searching the Windows File System

The Windows search utility makes it easy to locate files quickly. It can search an entire hard drive in minutes as opposed to it taking you hours to accomplish the same task. It can also be used to focus searches based on the file name, file contents, and location of the file. This is a very powerful feature that gives you immediate access to the information you need.

1) In order to access the Windows search utility, take your pointer and place it over the **Start** icon and **Left-click** once.

2) **Scroll up** to the **Search** option and another menu will open to the right.

3) **Click** on the option that says **Files and Folders.** This can also be accomplished by holding down the **WINDOWS** key and hitting the **F** key at the same time.

4) This will open the Windows **Search utility** window. Once you see this box, you will note several options on the left side of the window. **Click** on the option for **All files and folders.**

5) Please note in the left window pane a **Blueish box** that has two text boxes and one **Pull-down** option. If you are looking for a *specific* file name, type it in the *top* text box. If you are looking for *data located within a file,* type the data in the *second* text box down. The **Pull-down** option is for telling Windows where to search. So you could search the entire hard drive or just one folder. If you want to choose a *specific drive,* or a *folder on a specific drive,* then you have to use the **Pull-down** and choose the **Browse** feature. This will allow you to browse the entire computer and all external drives connected to the computer to identify a specific drive or folder on a drive to search. That's powerful.

6) There is a top text box that identifies a **Search by file name.** A file name is broken into two parts, a filename and a file extension. MYLETTER.DOC is a good example because MYLETTER is

the filename and (.DOC) is the file extension, which identifies it as a Microsoft Word-formatted file. Now suppose you want to find all Microsoft Word documents on the hard drive. All you would do is place the following text in the top text box *.DOC. The (*) is a wildcard that means anything, while the (.DOC) means that you are looking for all files ending in (.DOC).

If, for example, you want to locate all .MPG files on the hard drive, all you would do is enter the following text into the top text box *.MPG. The Windows search utility will search for any file that ends with .MPG. The (*) indicates you don't care what the file name is at all. Now let's see how we would do a search for a file name and not worry about what the file extension name is. If you were searching for all files that began with MYSHOWER, you would place the following text in the top text box MYSHOWER.*. This might return the following files: MYSHOWER.DOC, MYSHOWER.MPG, and MYSHOWER.TIF. Please understand that MYSHOWER is different from MY SHOWER because of the space between the *Y* and the *S*.

7) If you cannot remember the file name for a specific file, but you remember some of the text that is located in that file, you can use the second text box for the search. By leaving the top text box empty, you are telling Windows that you don't care what the file name is or what the file extension name is, but you are looking for text located within the file. So for the purposes of this exercise, let's assume you wrote a letter to someone who lived at 123 Main Street and you wanted to find that letter. All you would have to do is enter the text **123 Main Street** into the second text box and **Click** on the **Search** key. It would identify all documents that contained that data. For the purposes of all these searches, Windows does not distinguish between lower case and capital letters. So there is no difference between 123 MAIN STREET and 123 main street.

8) Now let's get a little tricky by creating a complex search. In the top text box, type ***.doc** and in the second text box type **123**

Main Street. This would locate all Microsoft Word documents that had 123 Main Street in the contents of the document. Wow, it's getting easier! I didn't have to ask you that time, because I knew you would know the answer. Practice this a few times before moving on because this is going to be key to review large amounts of data very quickly.

Deleted File Recovery

How do you get rid of a file when we want to? All you have to do is simply **Delete** the file and that lets the Windows file system know that the file is no longer needed. However, the confusion for the novice computer user is in the word *delete.* One would think that to delete a file means to destroy the file; not so with computers. The Windows file system will "un-reserve" that space, and that space becomes available for new data that is written to the hard drive. So, in actuality, deleting a file means to simply un-reserve the space that it occupies on the hard drive and make that space available to newer files.

Due to the combination of certain criteria that include the size of the hard drive, how the Windows file system writes to the drive, and the location of the deleted files, deleted files can remain on a hard drive for an extended time before they are overwritten through the natural progression of normal system usage. These deleted files can sit on a hard drive for days, weeks, months, and even years without being over-written. Contrary to what a novice would believe, the data is never deleted. What happens is the space that it occupies has been marked un-reserved, but the data is still there. Wow!

In order to recover the deleted data, a utility is used to search for and then re-reserve the space that the file occupies and presto, we have un-deleted (restored) the files. By now, you know that it was never really gone in the first place. I can tell you from my experience that more often than not, deleted files have a good chance of lasting years on a home computer, unless someone has taken the overt action to over-write or shred the deleted file space. In several of my cases, I have found files indicating that the spouse has been carrying on multiple affairs for many years. The files that contained the communications were all thought to have been deleted (due to the cheating spouse's lack of understanding of technology), but remained on the hard drive waiting to be recovered. It's that simple.

Understanding Files, Dates, and Times

This will most likely be one of the most important portions of this book if you need to understand how to decipher file dates and times. A forensic expert could review the file structure of a computer and easily determine what you were doing and when you were doing it. All of this information is compiled by reviewing files and their attributes. A file attribute includes information such as file name, file dates, times, and size. Did you know that a file has many file dates and times? These dates include file created date, file last modified date, file last accessed date, and – in some cases – the file date of deletion.

You may have to read this section a few times because to some people, understandably it can be very confusing. When you see the list of files in Windows Explorer and you choose the **Details view** option, you will see many of the attributes assigned to those files.

Let's say you create a word-processing document on December 24, 2005. The file creation date will be December 24, 2005, the file last modified date will be December 24, 2005, and the file last accessed date will be December 24, 2005. Now let's say you open this file again on December 31, 2005. All you did was open it in order to read it, and you simply **Closed** the document **Without clicking** on the **Save** button. The file creation date will remain December 24, 2005, the file last modified date will remain December 24, 2005, but the file last accessed date will changed to December 31, 2005. Remember, all you did was access the document file and that is why that one date changed. So far it's easy, right? Great!

If you now open the document on January 2, 2006, made modifications to the document, and then saved those changes, the file creation date will remain December 24, 2005, but the file last modified and the file last accessed dates will be changed to January 2, 2006. Remember, you accessed the document and then you modified the document so both of these dates changed. So far so good, right? Great!

Here is where it gets a little tricky. Let's say you now copy that file from your hard drive to another hard drive, or even a USB drive, on January 14, 2006. Here is a good time to tell you that when you move files to a new media, the date the file was moved to that new media becomes its new file creation date. This is because it is the date that the particular file was created on that media and not necessarily the date the file was created with the word processor. That being said, the file creation date will be changed to January 14, 2006, the file last modified date will remain January 2, 2006, and the file last accessed date will change to January 14, 2006.

Before I explain a little more about this, let's review the file dates. If an individual who is not experienced in computer forensics would review these dates, they would either be confused or convinced that some nefarious activity had taken place. One could rightfully ask, "How could a document be created on January 14, 2006, but be last modified on January 2, 2006?" In other words, how could it be modified before it was created?

So you are now thinking to yourself, *I'm pretty sure I understand everything so far but how did the file last accessed date change if I all did was copy the file using Windows Explorer and I did not open it?* I think this is a good time to explain a little more about accessing a file. Remember, I mentioned that when you open a file and **Do not click** on the **Save** button, and then you **Close** the document, the last modified date will not change but the last accessed date will. This also occurs when you **Click** on the file and then **Drag and drop** it to a new media.

As far as Windows is concerned, when you simply **Clicked** on that file, you accessed the file even if you did not open it. This is why it is very important *NOT* to go snooping around a computer when you plan to have a forensic expert acquire and analyze the hard drive. Your snooping will easily change key file dates and times, which will end up ruining your evidence and potential day in court. File dates and times can be tricky, but they are often key in a court of law. They help the court to determine the facts in a specific case and can often determine the outcome.

Now that you know all there is to know about file dates and times, it is time to discuss what impact copying files to a USB drive will have on the data. Please think about what you just read as we both go through this together. When you copy files from one drive to another, the file created date and the file last accessed date change to the current date and time, right? So your dates will *not* be the same as they are on your spouse's hard drive. But that's okay.

Keep in mind why you are looking at this data. Reviewing this data gives you the ability to conduct an early assessment of what you may want to do in the future, so it is a step in the planning process and the dates don't matter at this point. Here is the only thing that matters: *Is your spouse visiting dating, cheating, or other sites that you believe are inappropriate?* Reviewing the contents of your spouse's PROFILE folder will also tell you if they are taking extra steps to cover their tracks.

I recommend that you always *image a drive before you copy files from that drive,* but this book is designed to work the way you have decided to proceed. Everyone has a different set of circumstances, budgets, and goals and objectives. Remember, all you may need is to see the information before you decide to perform an in-depth analysis, which might also help you start to plan for your future. *No matter what you see, please do not make any rash decisions without fully understanding the meaning of what you found and before consulting with a lawyer.*

Windows Properties Feature

The Windows properties feature provides important information that can be useful in many instances. Almost every part of the Windows operating system and file system has properties including files, folders and desktop icons just to name a few.

The **Properties** screen for any Windows object provides information, which includes the name of the object, the type, the location, the logical size, the physical size on the disk, data it contains (if relevant), date created, last modified date, and the last accessed date. A Windows object can be a folder, file, **Desktop** icon, or just about any part of the Windows system. This feature is important in determining the installation date of an application, the file creation date of specific profiles, folders, or files, and the size of specific folders or files.

It is important to understand how file dates and times are easily affected, which will be covered shortly. This is the only way you will be sure that the information you are looking at is correct. For example, if you copied folders or files from the hard drive onto a USB drive and then looked at the properties, the file creation date would be the date that you copied the files to the USB drive, not the original date of that object.

So if you are looking for actual installation dates and you have not imaged the drive you would have to view the properties of the folder or file while it was on your spouse's computer. Remember that the last accessed date will also be changed to the current date because you are currently accessing it to view the properties. If you copied the folder or files to a USB drive and you then reviewed the properties of the folders or files on the USB drive, you would be looking at incorrect information as it relates to the dates and times of that specific Windows object. However, don't worry about the file dates and times right now as you will be reading and learning about them very shortly. I wanted to give you an early warning of the importance of this topic and why you need to know more about them.

In order to find the properties of any Windows object you can begin by starting Windows Explorer.

1) In order to access Windows Explorer, hold down the **WINDOWS** key and then depress the **E** key at the same time. This will open the Windows Explorer window.

2) **Click** on the **(+)** sign to the left of the **(C:)** and this will expand the WINDOWS FILE TREE under the **(C:)** drive.

3) **Scroll down** and **Expand** the DOCUMENTS AND SETTINGS folder, which will reveal all the PROFILE folders

4) Highlight the PROFILE folder you want to practice on and then using your mouse, **Right-click.** This will bring up a small menu.

5) I want you to **Scroll down** to the bottom of that menu to the **Properties** option and **Left-click** once on **Properties.** This will bring up the **Properties** screen. This screen has all the relevant information you will be looking for regarding that object.

This exercise certainly demonstrates the importance of the forensic process because you see how easy it is to inadvertently modify the dates and times of any Windows object. However, this is why you need to assess your specific situation first. If you are just looking for e-mail to quickly access if your spouse is cheating, then copying the e-mail files to a USB drive and reviewing the contents at another location will accomplish that objective. The dates and times of the e-mail files will not matter, as discussed earlier in this book, as they have bearing on the dates and times of the messages contained in those files.

The **Properties** feature will also be used to determine what size USB drive you need to copy files to. If you are just after the information contained in a specific profile, then all you have to do is **Highlight** that PROFILE folder and follow the instructions above to obtain the size of the specific PROFILE folder. If you want to copy all PROFILE folders, then you need to highlight the DOCUMENTS AND SETTINGS folder and obtain the **Properties** for that specific folder.

This powerful feature can be used to determine when a file shredder was installed or when an e-mail profile was created. Now that you know the importance of this feature, I am sure you have many uses for it. When used properly, it can provide a great timeline of your spouse's online activities.

6

Analyzing Computers

Computer Forensic Process

The goal of this chapter is to provide you with the knowledge and methodology necessary to successfully acquire an image of a computer hard drive and then to analyze that image to locate and retrieve the information you need to make decisions. It is important that you need to know exactly *what* you are doing and *how* you are going to accomplish it.

In the computer forensics industry, there are many individuals who know how to hook up a hard drive, start an application, and image a drive, but have absolutely no idea what is taking place during the process. In fact, their lack of knowledge is exposed when and if their case ever goes to court. I know you're not an expert; but since I am teaching you, I want you to be better than some professionals who do this full time. This is a worthwhile goal to achieve.

In order to reach that goal, it is necessary to introduce you to the concepts, processes, and terminology of computer forensics. These concepts and processes will enable you to adhere to a methodology that will ensure that you are the most successful you can be in protecting and recovering information. The best place to start is to explain the process that an expert goes through when they perform computer forensics.

This may seem very complex and complicated to some readers, but this is not the process that you will have to *perform.* I am providing you this information so you will know *how* it should be done; that's all. It is important, so read through the next few pages and don't worry about retaining the information. The more you hear it, the more the facts will sink in. It is not going to be difficult.

The first task at hand is to get the computer into our custody. When a client brings the computer into our lab, we have forms that our technicians complete to help us identify the computer and its components. This information includes the make, model, and serial number of the computer. We also note any and all devices that the computer has installed, which may include a DVD or Zip drive, etc. After we have documented all of the necessary information, we then take still pictures of the computer. This not only helps to support our documentation, but also aids in establishing the condition of the equipment at the time we accepted it into our custody.

The next step is to remove the hard drive from the computer and document the make, model, and serial number of the hard drive(s) that were removed from the computer housing. A still picture is then taken of the hard drive(s), which depicts the label that contains all of the manufacturer's information relevant to that hard drive(s), including the serial number.

The hard drive is then connected to a device called a write-blocker. The write-blocker is then connected to our forensic computer. The purpose of the write-blocker is to protect the hard drive. The write-blocker allows the forensic computer to access the hard drive and read information from the target hard drive that the client brought in, but it does not allow the forensic computer to write information to that hard drive. This ensures that the evidence collected by the forensic technician is not tampered with, and it helps establish the credability of the evidence later in court proceedings if necessary.

The forensic computer is then booted up to its own internal hard drive or the target drive is connected to the forensic computer via some type of *hot swappable connection.* A hot swappable connection simply means that we can connect a hard drive to the computer without turning the computer **OFF** and **Rebooting.** This can be accomplished by connecting the write-blocker (which is attached to the hard drive) to a USB or firewire port on the forensic computer. As soon as the hard drive is connected, the computer recognizes the drive.

The forensic technician then executes a program that will be used to create a bit stream image of the target hard drive. The term *bit stream image* means that it produces an exact duplicate of the hard drive, which not only includes the entire file system, but also the un-partitioned, unallocated, and deleted areas of the hard drive. It is an exact duplicate of the system hard drive and it is no different than having the drive itself.

The bit stream image is not a backup of the computer's file system. In fact, there is a major difference between a typical file backup and creating a bit stream image. While most backup systems use the operating system of the computer to archive all or selected files on the computer, the process of creating a bit stream image does not rely on the operating system that is installed on the target hard drive.

The process of creating a bit stream image actually ignores the operating system and copies physical sectors of the hard drive sequentially until it has imaged every sector located on that hard drive. This is what enables you to later gain access to the deleted files that are no longer part of the file system of the computer. A typical backup of a file system will not get you what you need, so don't be tempted to listen to others who are not experts, as you may be missing a great deal of the information you need to review.

The integrity of the entire bit stream image is maintained by the use of a *one-way numeric hashing calculation* to produce *a message digest,* which serves as a *digital fingerprint* for that file. The integrity of a bit stream image ensures that the evidence file has not been tampered with. When you create a bit stream image of your spouse's computer, every evidence file that is created has a digital fingerprint. The total of all evidence files make up the contents of your spouse's hard drive. I don't want to get too technical, but basically a numeric calculation is performed on the contents of the hard drive, and the numeric result of that calculation serves as the digital fingerprint. So let's say that numeric value is 73743840324343443876. Once the bit stream image is complete, the same calculation is performed on the contents of the image file created as a result of the imaging process, which also produces a numeric value of 73743840324343443876. They should match to have a successful image. If the image was different by just one character or a space between two letters, the value might look like this: 89776840111353449976. Now you can see how just one small change would be reflected in the digital fingerprint. This would mean that something happened during the image process or that someone tampered with the file.

These values serve as a digital fingerprint for that specific file. If the numeric values match, the bit stream image was successful and this match proves that the image is an exact duplicate. If anything changed on that image due to corruption, or for any other reason, the values would be totally different. This value is then stored with the forensic image files. If anyone attempts to change or modify anything, this value will not match during future validations and that will show that someone may have attempted to modify the forensic image. Corruption can also cause an image to fail a validation if the image was on a computer that suffered a crash.

The data stored in the bit stream image can be written to one or more files on a separate hard drive. It is beneficial, however, to break the bit stream image up to files of 650 MB in size so, if necessary, they can be stored on CDs. Since most computers sold today are shipped with hard drives exceeding 60 gigabytes, the forensic bit stream images can take up a lot of hard-drive space.

In our lab, we store images to a multiple terabyte server and still find we need to delete the images almost immediately after the case has been completed. Many of these images would take up to forty CDs to store them, if there was a need to save them for any length of time. The downside to CD storage is that if any one of the images became corrupt or if any one of the CDs was scratched, the forensic bit stream image would be useless. If it is important that the images are preserved for any length of time, it is imperative that they are well cared for.

The hard drive is then removed from the write-blocker and placed back into the original computer. Depending on the case, the computer is either returned to its owner or placed into evidence and retained as original until otherwise determined by the courts or legal counsel. All of the forensic analysis would then be performed on the bit stream image. Remember, the bit stream image is an exact duplicate and, using a forensic software utility, it can be accessed just as simply as you would access the hard drive itself. The major benefit is that it is read-only and can only be viewed, so there is no chance of anything being added or modified. This ensures the integrity of the forensic process and enables the forensic technician to search, access, and review data without modifying potential evidence.

Preparing to Image a Drive

If you have read every word in every chapter up to this section, then I am very proud of you. It may have taken some time and you may have even burned out some brain cells during the process, but the information in all the previous chapters is very important if you want to be successful. Now that you've learned all you need to know and have seen a high-level view of how the pros do it, how different and difficult is the process you have to use? I can tell you that it is not difficult at all, so let's get started.

I am going to cover a few things that need to be reinforced at this point so you don't have any problems and there are no misunderstandings. First, I am assuming that you have the legal right to access and image the hard drive of the computer you are about to image. Second, never copy anything to the hard drive of the computer you want to image. This includes installing software. If you do copy anything to this computer, you will overwrite areas of the hard drive that may contain data. So, in essence, you may be destroying the very data you are attempting to recover.

The first thing you need to determine is your level of access to the computer. There are three potential levels of access that you might have: no access, limited access, or administrative access. If you do not have access to a USERNAME and PASSWORD and you can't get past the USERNAME AND PASSWORD prompt, then you have no access.

If you have limited access, then you will not be able to image the entire hard drive. I walked you though the process of determining if you have limited access in Chapter 4. If you don't know if you have limited or administrative access, then please go back to that chapter and complete the steps necessary before continuing with this chapter. If you know that you have administrative access, then you may proceed in this chapter.

There are a few items that you will need to accomplish this process. First you will need a computer to work on that is *not* the same computer that you want to image. This can be a friend or relative's computer, but never the computer you want to image. (You may notice that I keep repeating that. It is important, and I don't want you to forget it.)

If you don't have a friend who has a computer that you can use, then you need to consider buying a used computer from a local computer store that sells used or refurbished computers. I would recommend something like an IBM T21 or any laptop computer that works correctly, has at least one or two USB ports, 256 MB RAM, and a 20 GB hard drive. They range in cost between $100.00 and $500.00 and can also be found on eBay. Find a good computer at the best price.

A laptop computer enables you to be mobile, and it is also easy to store – hopefully where your spouse will not see it. I don't want you to be in a position where your spouse asks, "What is this computer doing here?" and your response would be, "Oh, that's my forensic computer, Dear. By the way, where is your cell phone?" Remember what I said earlier in the book about being discreet.

You will also need a USB hard drive to store the applications that you need to use, as well as the forensic images that will be created as a result of you imaging your spouse's hard drive. The USB drive is an external hard drive that can store data and are sold in different capacities that range from 128 megabytes to 500 gigabytes. Also, you will need the application that enables you to image your spouse's hard drive.

I nicknamed the USB "Unfaithful Spouse Buster" because of the power and physical size of the USB drive; although USB is really an acronym for Universal Serial Bus, yet another technical term most likely named by a computer geek. External hard drives are also sold with firewire connections. If you buy one of these, make sure it also has a USB connection. The reason is that almost every computer has a USB port, but few have firewire ports. Please make sure you know what you are buying so you don't have to purchase additional equipment to fix the issues created by not buying the correct device in the first place.

The 128 MB USB drive can fit into the palm of your hand, while the 500 GB USB drive will take a desk drawer to store. The drive I recommend that you use is made by IO Magic and is an 80 gigabyte external hard drive that can fit into a purse or the inside pocket of a sports coat. The last time I checked the drive was selling for under $200.00. The other great part about this USB drive is that it does not have a power cord as it is powered off the USB port of the computer, which makes it easier to carry and store.

You can purchase any USB drive you want. I do recommend that you purchase a small physical USB drive that has plenty of storage capacity. If you don't, you will not be able to image the drive successfully because you will run out of storage room.

This is a great time to make sure what size hard drive your computer has. Please determine the drive size before you purchase any USB hard drive. Remember, some hard drives in personal computers are as large as 80 gigabytes so to be on the safe side you may need a USB drive that is at least 100 gigabytes.

Once you have the USB external drive, you are ready to download and store the application that you are going to need to image your spouse's hard drive. *Never use the computer you want to image to perform any work on.* Go to a friend's house or gain access to another computer that has high-speed Internet access and attach the external USB drive to that computer. High-speed Internet access is DSL or cable, and should take you three to five minutes to download the application.

Several companies make applications that enable you to image a hard drive. If you are aware of a certain application, please feel free to use it. I have chosen FTK Imager for the example here because it was published by a company that is owned by one of the foremost decryption experts in the country and whose company is a tremendous resource in field of computer forensics.

FTK Imager Software

FTK Imager will not only allow you to image the drive, but it will also allow you to preview the drive in a Windows Explorer-type of environment, while protecting the contents of the drive. This is why it is important for you to know how to navigate Windows — it will make using this application a lot easier. If you had the time, you could browse through the Web cache, e-mail, and other items.

If your goal is to image the drive, then I highly recommend that you focus on doing that first. When you know that you will have some time alone, you can *review* the image of the drive. Remember, the image is an exact duplicate of the drive, so you will have everything that is on that drive. Since you don't need the drive anymore, get the image and then take the USB drive off the computer and review the image when you have more time. It may be best to do this at a different location, like at a friend's home. I have had cases when spouses have been caught in the act of reviewing the drive, resulting in confrontations with their cheating spouses.

The FTK Imager demo version will allow you to image the drive and look around, but that is where the features end. If your goal was to get an image before you lost access to the hard drive because your spouse was moving out and you wanted a copy before they left, then there is no need to purchase the product — at least not yet. I would focus on getting the image of the hard drive with the free demo version and *preview* the hard drive to see what you can determine. Then decide to purchase the full-featured product if you want to proceed past the initial review with some powerful searching features.

The product you will end up purchasing is called FTK, an acronym for Forensic Tool Kit, and purchasing the product does have its benefits. The most important reason that most people purchase the application is to get access to a full-featured and powerful application that is not available in the demo version. People also purchase products for technical support in case they end up having problems with the application. In addition, as an application owner you may also have access to future updates as they become available. *Please make sure that if you purchase the product that you do not use your own credit card as your spouse may notice the purchase on the monthly statement.* Have a friend purchase it for you under your name but using their credit card.

The FTK full-featured product is an application that has to be installed and should never be installed on the target computer, which is the computer you want to image. So getting access to another computer is going to be important. While FTK is a product that sells for over $1,000.00, the company is currently working on developing a product that will allow you to image and analyze one hard drive for a cost that is approximately $149.00, which I am sure will be subject to change.

For the purposes of this chapter, we will be using the free demo version. You should be able to download this application from the Access Data website, which is located at http://www.accessdata.com/support/downloads/. This URL is Access Data's download section for all of their products. The name you need to look for is "FTK Imager: Minimum Files Necessary to Run Program – No Installation Required." This is very important, as there are two Windows versions of the software. One version requires installation and the other version provides individual files that can be copied to a USB drive and run without installation. *Make sure to look for the version that* does not *require installation. It will be identified that way on their website.*

1) Create a folder on the USB drive and name it FTK IMAGER.

2) Place the APPLICATION files in that folder on the USB drive.

Keeping your application utilities on the same drive as the images of your spouse's computer makes it easier to keep track of things as they are all together. This is true, especially if they are kept on a nice small and sleek hard drive that is easy to carry, conceal, and store.

Imaging the Hard Drive

There are two ways to image the hard drive using the FTK Imager, depending on which version of the product you are using. The first version we will discuss is the product that runs on a Linux® CD, which you will boot to. If you purchased the Access Data CD to change your access rights, then the FTK Imager is also loaded on that same CD. The second product is a Windows version that will run from the external USB drive. This is the version that has a free demo that you can use. The Linux CD must be purchased from the Access Data Corporation. This chapter will discuss both so you may choose to jump to the section that explains how to use the Linux version or to the section that explains how to use the free Windows demo version.

The Linux CD that you purchased from Access Data makes imaging hard drives simple, but there are a few things that you should know. First, not every computer will work with the Linux CD. It will all depend on the make and model of the computer you want to image as well as the external USB hard drive that you purchased. When it comes down to it, Linux will not work well with some hardware components or the software that makes them work — referred to as *drivers*.

The second issue is that Linux cannot use all of the computer's resources — as Windows does — so using Linux is slower than imaging a hard drive using the Windows version. If you have the time and the boot CD works with your equipment, Linux is the easiest way to proceed. You will, though, still need the Windows version to open the images and review your spouse's hard drive.

FTK Imager Linux CD Version

Let's start the imaging process using the Linux bootable CD. I just want to point out that Linux is an operating system that has nothing to do with the Windows operating system. In some cases, it can be more versatile than Windows, which is why it is often used with these types of utilities. It will not look like a Windows environment and some of your keys, as well as your mouse, may not work with Linux. You can still navigate your way around using the **ARROW** keys, as well as others, as we proceed.

1) Place the Linux bootable CD into the target computer's CD drive.

2) Connect the USB external hard drive to your target computer and **Power on** the computer.

3) If all goes well, the computer will boot to the Linux CD and you will see a screen that is titled **Access Data FTK Imager** and **XPAccess** centered at the top of the screen.

4) There will also be three menu options, **Image a hard drive, Modify login access,** and **Change login password.**

5) Highlight **Option 1** using the **ARROW** keys and then hit **ENTER** or the **SPACE BAR**.

6) This will bring you to a menu page that requires you to fill in the appropriate answers in order to image your spouse's computer successfully. Don't panic if it seems complex. I will walk you through the process explaining every option as we go.

The first option that you are required to answer is titled **Source the drive being imaged.** The source drive is the drive you want to image (on the target computer). Since you are working on the computer that you want to image, it will be called a **Primary drive.** If you see more than one **Primary drive** as you go through the list, this means that your spouse has more than one physical drive in the computer. If this is the case, then you have to come back later and image the second drive as well. For the purposes of this exercise, we will assume that there is only one primary drive listed.

7) **Highlight** the **Source the driving being imaged** option.

8) **Scroll** through the available source drives that are listed for that option.

9) When all is said and done, I want you to then select the **Primary hard drive1.** There may be data like (/dev/hda1) or something similar just to the right of **Primary hard drive1,** as this is Linux wording for the same thing.

10) The second option is the **Destination** drive. This is where you want to store the evidence image files when they are created. *It is important that you make sure that you choose the correct*

drive. Since you already chose the **Primary hard drive1** for the source, this drive should have been taken out of the listing and you should now see only **External hard drive1.**

11) If you don't see anything, there is a problem with Linux recognizing the USB drive and you may have to image the hard drive using the Windows version. Remember, I mentioned that Linux may not recognize certain devices or software drivers. If you purchased the product, you may also contact technical support but I think they may tell you the same thing. For this exercise, I am assuming that everything went okay, so choose the **External hard drive1** as the destination and let's move on.

12) The next option asks for a DESTINATION folder. This is just a folder to store the image files in. However, the folder must already exist, as the application will not make one if you just type a name there. **Let's leave this just as it is** or you will have problems.

13) You will now be asked for a FILE NAME. This is the name you want to call the image files. You might want to name it by the date so you know by looking at the files what date you imaged the computer's hard drive or by what device you imaged, such as computer or laptop. You can name it 0406LAPTOP, or whatever name you like. So **type a name in here** and let's move on.

14) The next option asks what **Type of image file** you want to create. In the field of computer forensics, there are several different image file types that an expert often uses. For the purposes of what you need to accomplish, I want you to stay with the **Default** setting, which should be **E01.** If this is not the default setting, then change the option and set it to **E01.**

15) You will also see an option to **Set compression** (just to the right of the **Image file type**). This is a setting that will help reduce the size of the image files you create to help save space on your hard drive. While adding compression will take a little longer to create the image files, it is best to leave this at the **Default** setting.

16) **Segment size** option is next. This should be set to **650MB** as the **Default** setting. If so, then just **leave this as it is.** The hard drive is a very big storage device and the application would create one big massive file if we let it. By keeping this setting at 650MB, the application will create one IMAGE file at a time keeping the size of each file to 650MB. A typical drive will result in creating between five and forty IMAGE files. All of the combined files make up your spouse's hard drive. It is now possible to store each IMAGE file on a CD-ROM, if necessary. This may not be very convenient, but it will certainly make it easier to keep copies safe.

17) **Setting the image verification** is the next option. By default, the setting should be set **ON.** If you **have time** to image the drive and verify the drive, then **keep this setting as it is.**

Verifying the image will add a significant amount of time to the process, so if you **don't have the extra time,** then set this to **OFF.**

The next time you open the image files using the FTK Imager, it will go through the verify process then. If it does not complete successfully, you can always go back and try again. If needed, you can also review the data even if the image does not verify properly. I have, however, had this happen to me only once in my entire career and it was due to drive corruption.

18) At the bottom of the screen, you should see the wording **Start image process. Highlight Start image process** and then hit the **ENTER** key to start the process. You are now imaging your spouse's computer and are just a few short hours away from having an exact copy of what is on that drive. Congratulations. I knew you would be able to do this.

19) When the imaging process has been completed, **Exit** the application and turn **OFF** the computer. **Wait until the computer is powered down before disconnecting the external hard drive.**

20) Clean up the area around the computer so it is not apparent that you were working there and walk away with the evidence image files on your USB hard drive. Please make sure that you reverse any security-level modifications that you made to get access to the computer, or your spouse may notice.

21) The next step would be to analyze the image files using another computer, which will be covered in the section after the next.

FTK Imager Windows Version

The Windows version of FTK Imager is often used for two reasons: When the Linux CD version does not recognize devices or hardware drivers; or, when speed is an issue and you need to complete the imaging much faster. The Windows version also will enable you to easily review the image in a Windows Explorer environment once you have completed the imaging of the target hard drive.

1) The first step is to get the Windows version of the FTK Imager loaded on the external USB drive that you purchased. There are two versions available. The first version requires you to install the application on the target computer. *Don't use this version.* Make sure you *ask for the version that allows you to simply place a few files on an external USB drive and then start the application from that external hard drive.*

2) Place the FTK Imager files in a folder called FTK IMAGER so you will always know where they are. This helps keep you organized. Once you have completed this step, you are ready to proceed.

3) **Start** your spouse's computer and let it boot up.

4) **Login** with an account that has ADMINISTRATIVE access.

5) Once you are logged in, attach the external USB hard drive to the computer and let the computer recognize it.

6) A small window may appear showing you the contents of that external hard drive but just close that window using the **X** at the top right of that window.

7) Now take your pointer and bring it down to the **Start** button on the screen.

8) **Right-click** on top of the **Start** button and a menu will appear.

9) **Highlight** the menu option titled **Explore** and then **Left-click** once on that option.

10) This will cause the **Windows Explorer** window to appear and you can use this to navigate your way to the external hard drive. Remember that you also can accomplish this by holding down the **WINDOWS** key and depressing the **E** key.

11) The external hard drive that you connected to the computer should be visible in the left window pane toward the bottom of the listing and may appear as **Local Disk (D:), Removable Disk (D:), or Public (D:).** The actual letter may be any letter starting with *D* and moving higher in the alphabet.

12) If you **highlight** the external drive, you should see the FTK IMAGER folder that you created before you started this process. **Double-click** on that folder. That folder will open and you will see all the files inside the folder.

13) The file will be named FTK IMAGER and it should have an icon that looks like a magnifying glass. I want you to **Double-click** on that icon and the application will start.

14) Once the application starts, you will see an **Application** window appear. **Click** on the **File** option, located at the top left of that window.

15) **Scroll down** to the option titled **Create disk image.**

16) **Clicking** this option will open a smaller window titled **Select source.** This is where you identify what type of device you

want to image. The default setting is PHYSICAL DRIVE and this is the correct setting.

17) **Click** on the NEXT icon located at the bottom of the small window.

18) The next window should be titled **Select drive,** which means the source drive because we just set the source drive type. Remember: *The source drive is the hard drive that you want to image.* Since you are using the target computer it should be PHYSICAL DRIVE0.

18) Use the **Pull-down** option just to see what other drives are listed there. Then keep the **Default** setting if it is set to PHYS-ICAL DRIVE0.

19) **Click** on the **Finish** icon located at the bottom of the window.

20) This will take you to a window that is titled **Create image.** You will note that the source drive is listed toward the top as \.\\PHYSICAL DRIVE0. There is a box below that is titled **Image destination**. I want you to **Click** on the **Add** icon and it will bring you to another window that is asking for what type of image file you want to create.

21) The forensic industry uses several types of forensic image files, but I want you to make sure that you **Check** the **E01** file type. It should be the bottom choice, so make sure you **Click** on that option and the circle fills in for that option. The E01 image file type is an industry-accepted standard that will allow you − or any other expert that you may want to send them to in order to get the opinion of an independent third-party expert − to analyze the image files. Choose the E01 file type and **Click** on the **Next** icon at the bottom of the window.

22) You will now see a window titled **Evidence item information.** This is used by experts to document the specifics of each case. I would recommend that you fill them in with the same type of identifying information that experts use. I typically **name a**

case by the date and then add a 100 at the end so I can start counting other cases that we get on the same date as 060401100. You can simply call it **spouse0406** (husband or wife). Fill in the rest of the information and list your name as the examiner. Then hit the **Next** icon located at the bottom of the window.

23) The next window is titled **Select image destination.** The top option is asking for a DESTINATION folder, but what it is really asking for is not only a folder, but also the drive. I want you to use the **Browse** icon just to the right of the empty text box and **Navigate** your way to the external USB drive. This should be **(D:)** or a higher letter in the alphabet. This will depend on whether or not you have a CD-ROM installed, as well as other types of drives, including ZIP drives. Make sure that you see the FTK IMAGER folder on that drive. This will ensure that you are using the correct drive as the designation drive. (Remember that the destination drive is where you want to store the image files that are created. Please pay close attention when selecting this option.)

24) The next option below the DESTINATION folder is asking you to name the files that you want created. I would recommend that you **name it by the date for now.** For example 060401 for April 1, 2006, or call it whatever you want that makes it easy to understand. Leave the rest of the setting as they are and then **Click** on the **Finish** icon.

25) This will bring you back to the **Create image** window. All you have to do now is **Click** on the **Start** icon and the imaging process will begin.

26) A window will open that is titled **Creating image.** This window will let you know the estimated time it will take to image the drive, as well as a status bar to let you know just how much has been completed. I used a 52 GB hard drive to set up a demonstration in order to see how long it would take to image the

hard drive. The estimate for the 52 GB hard drive was three hours and twenty-two minutes. This time will depend on the power of the computer that you are using and the speed of the external hard drive you are writing the images to. Congratulations. I knew you would be able to do this.

While this image is being created, I would like you to jump to the section titled "Analyzing the Forensic Image."

27) When the imaging process has been completed, **Exit** the application and turn **OFF** the computer. **Wait until the computer is powered down before disconnecting the external hard drive.**

28) Clean up the area around the computer so it is not apparent that you were working there and walk away with the evidence image files on your USB hard drive. Please make sure that you reverse any security-level modifications that you made to get access to the computer or your spouse may notice.

The next step is to analyze the image files using another computer. This will be covered in the next section.

Analyzing the Forensic Image

The difficult – and potentially hectic – part of the process has been completed. You now have an image of your spouse's hard drive. Imaging a hard drive can not only be tricky, but it can be stressful because you are not a technical expert and you may be worried that your spouse may walk through the door at any time unannounced. It's over; you were successful; and from this point on, it will be easier because you will be able to control your environment. In other words, you can choose when and where you want to analyze the images. You don't have to analyze them at home, unless you feel comfortable knowing that you can perform that task and not be discovered. The choice is yours. I should also note that if you are in the middle of analyzing an image, you can simply shut everything off if you find out that your spouse is heading home.

1) The first thing you need to do is **Start up** the computer that you plan to use as your forensic computer (as opposed to the target, your spouse's, computer).

2) Once the forensic computer is running, attach the external hard drive to the computer.

3) Using Windows Explorer, **Navigate** your way down to the drive and open the FTK IMAGER file folder.

4) **Double-click** on the **FTK Imager** icon located in that folder, which will start the FTK Imager application.

5) **Click** on the **File** option, located at the top left side of the screen.

6) **Scroll down** to and **Click** on the menu option **Add evidence item.** If you did the imaging using the Windows version of FTK Imager, this window will look very familiar. The window is titled **Select source.** The last time you were at this screen you selected Physical drive. This time, **Select Image file.** The application is asking what to open and you want to tell it to open an image file that you created.

7) Once you select **Image file, Click** on the **Next** icon located at the bottom of the window.

8) The next window is titled **Select file.** This is the application asking you which image files you want to open. **Click** on the **Browse** button located on the screen to the right of the blank text box and **Navigate** your way to the external hard drive that is attached to your forensic computer.

9) As you view the files, you will notice that one of the files has an icon that is different from the others; it looks like small gray box. In addition, all of the other image files will have the ending of E02, E03, etc., but the **one that has a different graphic will not have this extension. That is the file you want to click on.**

10) It will take you back to the **Select file** window.

11) All you have to do now is **Click Finish,** which will import all of the image files into the application for analysis.

12) Toward the top left side of the screen, you will see the title **Evidence tree** just over the left window pane. Under that, you will see the case file that you named. This should have a plus **(+)** sign next to it. **Click** on the **Plus sign** and it will open the directory file structure of the imaged computer. You can **Start with Partition 1** and work your way down to the structure that is named **Root.** This is where all the files you need to get to are located.

13) Once you are here, it is like navigating the hard drive using Windows Explorer.

The Windows Explorer interface will enable you to browse the forensic image as though you were working directly on your spouse's hard drive. As you browse through the file and directory structure, you may notice that some of them have a red X through the file icon on the left side of the screen. These are the files that are marked as deleted but are still recognized by the Windows file system. These can be reviewed and restored as easily as any of the other files.

The best part is that as you browse and review all of the files they are being protected by the forensic software. Therefore all of the file dates and times will not be changed. You can also export these files to your external USB drive in order to print them out. Once you do, the file that was exported to your USB drive will no longer be protected and it will have its file date and time changed. The original copy of the file that is stored in the forensic image will always be protected by the forensic software.

The demo version of the FTK product that you are using also allows you to browse the unallocated space of the hard drive. You will notice that just below the ROOT folder there is a folder named UNAL-LOCATED SPACE. This space may contain graphic images, cached web-based e-mail messages, cached IM Chat messages and deleted Web pages plus so much more. However, it may take time for you to go through the entire space as in most cases there is a lot of hard drive space not currently allocated by the file system.

It is also possible to search for data located in the unallocated space of the hard drive using keywords but you need to purchase the full licensed version of the FTK software to use that feature. This feature will save you a lot of time and you will identify key information a lot quicker and more accurately. If you review the unallocated space manually, it will take you a lot longer and you may miss something. Remember, while this software is priced above $1,000.00 there is a special price of $149.00 offered by the Access Data Corporation for the analysis of one hard drive. You can continue to analyze one hard drive as many times as you want.

If you refer to the chapter on the Windows File System, you will find out where on the hard drive the files you may be interested in reviewing are located. The FTK software will actually let you review the contents of the hard drive in a Windows Explorer environment by reviewing the file structure and viewing many of the IMAGE and DOCUMENT files. If you highlight any file or folder in the FTK Imager and then **Right-click** that file or folder, you can export it to your USB drive to review it with the appropriate file viewer.

Restoring a Folder

I will now walk you through the process of restoring a folder that contains about 90 percent of what you may be looking to review.

1) Highlight the DOCUMENTS AND SETTINGS folder located in the left window pane.

2) **Right-click** the folder and choose **Export files.**

3) You will now see a window that will enable you to browse the system. **Browse** down to **your external hard drive.** You will know you are on the correct drive when you see the folder FTK IMAGER. **Click** on **Finish** and it will export the entire folder and subfolders to your external hard drive.

The DOCUMENTS AND SETTINGS folder holds all USER PROFILES, which in turn holds all the users' MyDocuments, MyPictures as well as all e-mail, Web cache, browser history, and favorites for all users of the system. Once you have this folder on the external hard drive, you will be able to use Windows Explorer and the Windows search utility to find and view files and so much more. You can also refer to the CyberLies.com website and check out our technical section for all updated information, such as our Technical FAQs, which will be made available to registered users of the site.

I want to remind you to think analytically here and remember that as you export files to your external USB hard drive for review, you are changing the dates and times of the files to the current date (the date you are now on the computer). However, you have a forensic image that is protecting all of the files and their attributes, so if a file date or time is important or you want to see when your spouse has been visiting certain sites, then all you have to do is look for those key files in FTK Imager and the original dates and times will be reflected there.

You also want to make sure that you read the chapter on Tools and Resources. This will cover different low-cost software and hardware products, as well as other important information that will help you locate even more information.

The important part of this whole process is that you now have image files of your spouse's computer. Once you have those image files and you need an expert's opinion, you can simply pick up the phone and call our office. We offer services to analyze image files created by our readers as well as system files exported by our readers (such as NTUSER.DAT), which can often contain user names and passwords to online Web portals where they have created their online personalities. Our readers can then obtain our services at a reduced rate by calling (888) 674-4872.

7

Cell Phones

Analyzing Cell Phones

Cell phones are the number one technology that most people own and use, and rely on almost every minute of their lives. Just think about it, we carry our cell phones with us no matter where we go. When we need to, we can place them on vibrate or even set them to silent altogether, but we would never imagine leaving them at home. Do we do this with our computers? The answer is no. Cell phones rule!

Cell phones have evolved into multifunctional devices by the merging of a variety of technologies such as Personal Digital Assistants (PDAs), which in turn store even more data. What a potential treasure-trove of information that is located within that device! Data in cell phones is more often than not a cornucopia of information that paints a clear picture of its user's activities. We literally use these phones for everything we do – including communicating with our boss, our clients, and our spouse. Something for you to remember is that a growing number of people use the same cell phone for communicating with their spouse, *and* the person with whom they are cheating.

Have you noticed that I have been using the word *communicate* instead of call? This is because cell phones now allow people to communicate in a number of ways. We can call each other no matter where we are in the world. What a powerful feature! We can also text-message each other by sending a short message from one phone to another; we can e-mail each other, and we can snap a picture and then send that picture to anyone we choose at the blink of an eye. Today, the number one preferred method to communicate while juggling multiple relationships is text-messaging, at least the "lovey-dovey" part . . . you know, those cute little messages that lovers send to each other and receive every minute of the day.

There are many reasons for this. First, these messages are the most personal because they are interactive and delivered directly to a person. Unlike e-mail, which is sent and received when the person is online at a later time, text-messages are real-time and you know that the other person is really there. Text-messaging provides a more exciting, personal connection between the two. Also, text-messages do not show up on the phone bill and, finally, they are fun to send and receive. For instance, they can be sent and received while the individuals are in meetings. What do you think your boss would say if you were speaking on the cell phone while they were talking? By keeping your cell phone below the conference table, you can carry on like a little kid. In fact, a growing number of people are doing just that.

Cell phones are now cameras. (I'll bet that you can't find a cell phone that is not a camera.) Who came up with that idea? It was brilliant! History tells us that if we find a great use for a device, there will always be people who figure a way to pervert its use. Thanks to them, cell phones are now being banned in many places because they have cameras. It started with a few perverts taking nude pictures of club members in sports' clubs. They took a quick picture and then sent it off to another pervert via that very same cell phone. That activity got the ball rolling on negative advertising and now they are banned in many places including schools, courts, and many other public places.

People are also taking pictures of themselves, their spouses, and others. They store and send these pictures; and when they are done with them, they delete them . . . or at least they think they are deleted. Are they? If you remember one thing remember this: *Nothing is gone forever when it comes to technology.* Most people have a total misunderstanding of technology and they use cell phones to do just about anything they want, believing that there is no way for anyone to find out what they have been doing. After all, they have the phone with them every minute of the day. Or do they?

There is nothing like a scorned spouse or partner to figure out a way to get to your cell phone as well as the data that is stored within. I have been involved in cases where people have done just that. Some of my clients have been successful and others have not. I can tell you that your level of success will always be proportionate to your level of knowledge and understanding you have about cell phones or any technology. So this chapter is going to be very important to you if you are interested in learning how to access cell phones to get the data you need to review. This book will provide the knowledge you need and all you have to add is the determination.

It is important to remember that most people take technology for granted. It's human nature that causes us to fall into a false sense of security, not to mention that most people underestimate the abilities of their spouse. Cheating spouses often think that no one has the ability to look at their cell phone because it is with them all the time; but is it? It is often these misconceptions that cause them to use their phone without discretion, which eventually may expose an affair if their spouse knows how to look at the information on the cell phone. Cell phones have a potential warehouse full of information, so knowing as much as you can about your spouse's cell phone is important.

There are so many manufacturers, makes, and models of cell phones and each has its own unique feature set, as well as methods of storing and accessing the information on each one. Then, just when you thought you knew all the latest phones and features, new models appear, new features are introduced, and they all work differently. So my point is that a little research, a little social engineering, and knowledge are going to be the key to your success.

The first step in achieving this goal is to find out everything you can about your partner's cell phone. You can do this by taking a look at it while they are sleeping. Make sure you record as much information as possible about the phone. If the manufacturer and model are not visible on the outside of the phone, then you will have to take out the battery, which is located under a removable panel on the back of the phone. When you do so, make sure to place the battery down and look at the information in the well of the phone where the battery used to reside. Some make the mistake and take the information off the back of the battery. That information is typically about the battery only and not the phone (although there are a few exceptions to that rule). Don't make that mistake or you may have to start all over again.

Now you need to know what features the phone has, how to use these features, and how to access the information that is stored on the device. You can accomplish this in one of two ways. You can track down the manual and read it inside and out, but that is not much use if you do not have the phone in front of you. When the manual tells you to hit a specific key and you don't have the phone in your hand, it is difficult to retain the information you are trying to learn. Searching for the information on the Internet is possible, but again without the phone in front of you, this will make learning and retention of the information harder.

Asking your partner to leave the phone at home so you can become familiar with its features is also out of the question. I think that will definitely raise their suspicions. I am going to ask you to think of an easy way to learn about the phone. I am asking you because I want you to start thinking about the resources available to you. I want you to start to develop an analytical mind as it relates to these types of activities. So don't cheat — stop here for a few minutes and think. If you have a good idea or if you tried and can't think of one, then start to read again.

Let's find the easiest way to get to know the phone. Have someone show you everything you need to know and, when you are not sure, ask them to explain it again. "How?" you ask. Go to the local phone store and ask if they have that make and model cell phone. If they do, then tell them you are very interested in purchasing that phone and you would like to find out as much as possible to make sure you like it and that it will meet your needs. Act like the good consumer and start with questions about specific features. This is called social engineering. Keep notes; and if they ask why you are writing things down, tell them to compare the features to other phones that you plan to look at.

If they tell you that the phone model is no longer available, then ask to see the model that replaced it. Never take their recommendation to go with a new cell phone that is made by a different manufacturer. Different manufacturers have different features and may have totally different ways of accessing the features and data. If you stay with the same manufacturer and just change the model, then you are more likely to find a phone that works in a manner similar to the one your spouse or partner uses.

Start with the features and ask the salesperson to tell you all the capabilities of the phone. Ask questions like, "How do I take a picture?" and, "How do I view all the pictures I have taken?" Have the sales associate take you through the logs and ask them to explain the purpose of each of the logs. Learn how to access all of the logs, as well as all text-messages (both sent and received), and learn how to send them. Act like you are interested in the phone and learn as much as you can in the process.

Then ask the associate about software to sync the phone to your computer and what they would recommend. *Sync software* enables you to take everything off the phone and place it on your computer and vice versa, but it does have its limitations. Record what sync software can be used with the phone, but don't buy anything yet. I mention this only because when you install software, it sometimes has default entries. These default entries would then be sent to your spouse's phone and if your spouse sees it there, it may raise their suspicions. So be careful. I will show you how to get around that when we talk about the various software products later in this chapter.

It is important to know about everything because only you can make the final decision on which way you want to proceed. This decision has to be based on your personal assessment of your own technical abilities. You may choose an easier path because you don't believe you can do something that, while it produces more information, it is also more challenging. The decision will be yours, so please pay attention so you can make the right decision. I don't want you to take an easy path if you are capable of doing more and getting more information in the long run.

Now that you have learned everything you need to know about your spouse/partner's cell phone, let's talk about the data that is stored on cell phones. A cell phone's primary use is as a telephone. We use this device to make and receive phone calls. Outgoing calls are made by dialing the number desired and then hitting the **SEND** button. When outgoing calls are made, regardless of whether or not they were successful, they are stored in a log that is accessible by the users.

This is a log that is typically identified as DIALED. If you were to access the DIALED log, you would see a listing of numbers that were dialed by that cell phone. If you **Scroll** to highlight any one of the numbers and then hit the **ENTER** button, you would gain access to different data fields. These fields of data include the NUMBER CALLED, a NAME if it was pre-programmed into the phone, the DATE AND TIME OF THE CALL, and the DURATION OF THE CALL. All of this is very important information. Where else do you think you could get the same information? You're right! Your cell phone bills. Remember that, because we will be coming back to that later when we discuss the cell phone bills.

There is also a log that is identified as RECEIVED. If you were to access the RECEIVED log, you would see a listing of numbers, which are the phone numbers of line and cell phones that have called that cell phone. A *line phone* is a house or business, because there are phone company lines running to their buildings. If you **Scroll** to highlight any one of the numbers and then hit the **ENTER** button, you would gain access to different data fields.

These fields of data include the ORIGINATING NUMBER (phone that dialed your spouse's cell phone), a NAME if pre-programmed into the phone, the DATE AND TIME OF THE CALL, and the DURATION OF THE CALL, all very important information. Where else do you think you could get the same information? You're right! (well, partially right). Your cell phone bills. Remember that, because we will be coming back to that later when we discuss the cell phone bills. I said *partially right* because not all the same information is available for inbound calls as it is for outbound calls on cell phone bills from all providers. Each service provider shows different information on their bills. In some cases, even the same cell phone service provider prints bills with different information based on the type of plan. It can be very confusing at times, but it is still very important information and you will soon find out why.

Once you have made the decision to start looking at your partner's cell phone, the best action plan is the simplest. You know your spouse's sleeping habits, so when they are in the middle of a deep sleep, take their cell phone and start to access and review the entire phone. If you have no way to download the data, write down everything you see, and store those records where you can retrieve them anytime you want. Remember to review and record everything.

You can also use software to download the information directly into your laptop computer. The software does have limitations and may not get everything off the cell phone. This topic will be covered later in the chapter. Writing the information on paper is the slowest and sometimes least accurate because you can make a mistake while writing, but at least you know you are recording all the information you see. Spouses sometimes use a combination of both software and pen-and-ink. By the way, if you are going to use a software product and start up a laptop computer in the middle of the night, make sure that the speaker is turned **OFF** and that you do the work far away from where your partner might be awakened by any noise.

After you take a look at the cell phone logs, take a look at the pictures, all the text-messages, and all the Quick Text listing. If your spouse is involved with another person, you may find a picture of that person or a text-message to or from that person, which was sent to the phone in any one of a number of ways, so make sure you look at everything.

The QUICK TEXT-MESSAGE listing is a listing of short pre-canned messages that you simply **Highlight** on your cell phone and then **Send** to the desired recipient. In other words, you don't have to type them in each time you want to text-message the person. Sometimes you will see messages like, "Love you," or, "Call you in 15 minutes." These messages are usually the default messages that came preprogrammed with the phone. It is important for you to know what the default Quick Text-Messages are so you will be able to differentiate them from the Quick Text-Messages that were added in by your spouse.

So if you see, "I love you Terry," and your name is not Terry, then this Quick Text-Message was added to the phone by your spouse. You can do this by making a list of the canned messages when you are at the phone store. This way, you will know the messages ahead of time and you will be able to pick out the new Quick Text-Messages that your spouse entered in after buying the cell phone. I can tell you that messages like "I love you Terry" do not come pre-programmed with the phone, which means that your spouse placed it there, which means that they may be involved in another relationship. As you look through the text-messages, be sure to record as much information as possible, including the originating number or e-mail address. Text-messages can be sent from other cell phones and also e-mail accounts.

Don't be tempted to analyze the data after you have copied it to paper or downloaded it to your computer. Get the cell phone back in its place and get to bed. There is plenty of time to do the analysis when it is safe and there is absolutely no chance of getting caught. Let me say that one more time: *Don't be tempted to analyze the data after you copied it to paper or downloaded it to your computer. Get the cell phone back in its place and get to bed.* You will thank me for that later. People have been caught by their spouse doing just that. Don't take chances, or you may end up losing the element of surprise and all the data you might have recovered may be gone, resulting in any future analysis being fruitless.

When reviewing the cell phone logs, it is important to remember that either of these logs can easily be deleted or altered, but that nothing can be edited. That means that individual log entries can be deleted, which alters the log; but the individual call transactions entries cannot be modified. For example, I can go into the DIALED log and start to **Delete** entries one at a time. I can be as selective as I want or I can just **Delete** all the entries. However, by deleting all of the logs, as a cheater I would raise the suspicion of my spouse, should they be checking my phone. So what do I do? I **Delete** only those entries that I feel are personal. So when the spouse looks at that data, it has been sanitized. That means that specific call transactions were deleted from the logs and no evidence of these calls has been left for anyone to find. This can happen to any log or data that is stored on that cell phone.

While your spouse may have made your job a little harder and more time-consuming, they have certainly helped you identify the numbers that are key to them and that are of clear evidentiary value. All you have to do is know what numbers they deleted. Easy right? Yes, it is easy. Remember those phone bills I told you about . . . now it's time to get them out. Once you have them, gather the phone logs that you have been keeping. You take the phone logs of what was in the phones DIALED directory and compare them to the cell phone bill OUTGOING calls for that same period. The dates and times will match to the minute.

Then start to **Highlight** those numbers that are on the cell phone bill but were not listed in the DIALED directory. If your spouse was deleting numbers from that listing, you've not only got them, but you now have additional information you didn't have before. (I love it when they totally misunderstand technology and end up making your life easier and wonder why they don't just tell you the numbers they called and get it over with.) Once you're done with this exercise, then you do the same for the RECEIVED logs. Again, **Highlighting** those entries that are on the cell phone bills but are not in the RECEIVED logs.

The RECEIVED logs are a little different. Depending on the cell phone service provider and the plan you have, there may be no numbers identified on the cell phone bill for the inbound calls. However, it would be good to know that there are inbound call transactions missing from the log but appearing on the cell phone bill. Note the date and time of the missing transactions that appear on the cell phone bill, since it might be useful information later on. If this occurs regularly, then you might see a pattern start to develop. If you have determined that your spouse has been deleting INCOMING call logs, even though you cannot determine the originating number, then that should raise your level of suspicion. They are deleting them for a reason.

I know that reviewing these logs and then comparing them to the cell phone bills is time-consuming and tedious . . . earlier I said it would be. It is useful, though, in that it may provide you a wealth of information without spending money. I also recognize that not everyone will have access to the cell phone bills for a number of reasons. The best way to proceed is to still record all of the information and then key in on the calls that had the longest durations. Then, work your way back to calls with the shortest durations. Then start to zero in on the early-evening timeframe when your spouse is not typically at home and yet most businesses and public places have closed. Look at all those numbers that are in the DIALED and RECEIVED logs that meet certain criteria and work from there. You know your spouse better than anyone, so improvise if you have to and you may get what you're looking for.

You can sometimes identify the owner of a phone number by searching for it online using one of the major search engines or even portals that provide reverse phone lookups. A *reverse phone number lookup* is when you type in a phone number to search for the subscriber, instead of using a name to find a number. If you go to your favorite search engine and enter the key phrase **Reverse phone search,** this will provide you with a listing of sites that may help you identify the subscriber of line phones, or enter the key phase **Reverse cell phone search.** This will provide you with a listing of sites that may help you identify the subscriber of a cell phone number.

I want you to do your best to make sure that the online company you are dealing with is reputable. I have heard complaints in the industry that some sites take your money and never get back in touch with you, while still others try to lead you into spending more money when the site never gave you anything to start with. A good rule of thumb is that if you do an inquiry with a site and they do not give you information, then don't give them any more of your money and try another site. The company may make it sound like your fault and by trying something different you might be successful. Don't fall for this ruse. Go to another site or just abandon the idea.

If all else fails and you want to see who is on the other end of a phone number, use a pay phone that is not near your home or work and just call the number. This is important to remember, as spouses often look at the caller ID. If they see that you might be calling, it will raise the suspicion of your spouse. In one of the cases that I was consulted on, a client found out that her husband had another cell phone that she did not know about. When she found it, she recorded the phone number. She then used a payphone in the area to call the cell phone. Her husband always let it go to VOICEMAIL, which was a generic computerized message. This made it impossible to see if he was really using the cell phone. She then went to the next step. She went to the area where she suspected his lover lived and used a pay phone from that area to call the number. How about that, her husband answered the phone and she quickly hung up. If you do this late at night or during the busy times of the day, you may just get the VOICEMAIL system and may not only hear the voice, but also the name of the subscriber. We all love to leave our names on the intro message that callers always hear.

Before I leave you, there are a few more things you need to know about cell phones that you may not be aware of. This knowledge may help to provide additional information that you can use to narrow down or key into specific timeframes. First, cell phones have the ability to be locked and then password protected. So if you pick up your spouse's cell phone, **don't turn it off** or you may find that you just locked yourself out.

Second, when someone calls a cell phone and the person is on the phone with another party, the person who calls the cell phone will hear beeps, which are designed to tell you that the person you are calling is on the phone with another party. Remember that because it might provide some crucial information that you may not have thought about. For example, you call your spouse and you hear the beeps telling you that they are on the phone. However, even though your spouse also hears beeps telling them that someone is calling, they may not place them on hold and pick up your call. They know who is calling because they can see it on the phone's caller ID. They may just let your call go to VOICEMAIL. Note the DATE AND TIME of this and check the phone bills to see the phone number/person they were talking with at that time. It may be nothing, but it may also be another lead for you and you may see a pattern start to develop during certain times of the day or certain days of the week. If you are organized and observant, you will start to notice these things happening if your spouse is involved with another person.

Spouses who are cheating sometimes have a hard time switching their train of thought and mood from talking to their "friend" to talking to their spouse. Their sense of guilt might give them away, so they just avoid the call from their spouse and may call them back later when they have a chance to regroup. That is not to say that every spouse is like that or that every time your spouse does not pick up your call, they are cheating on you. It is only meant to get you to start thinking about collecting information and then verifying it as you move forward. The more information you have, the easier it will be to determine if your spouse is cheating on you.

Third, cell phones are programmed and then follow that programming. One of the key features about the cell phone is the VOICEMAIL system. Therefore, it is important for you to become familiar with it. One programming feature you should be checking; is to **see how many rings it takes for the voicemail to normally pick up.** The best way to determine this would be to set your spouse's cell phone to vibrate or silent and then call your spouse's cell phone while they are sleeping. Count how many rings it takes before the VOICEMAIL system picks up. Try it twice and you will see it is the same number of rings each time. When you are done, *make sure to delete your phone number from your spouse's* RECEIVED *log.* If you don't, and they see it there, they may wonder why you are calling their phone in the middle of the night. Not good. *Also delete the numbers out of your phone's* DIALED *log,* just in case your spouse is checking your phone. This might provide some crucial information that you may not have thought about, so please remember it. For example, you call your spouse and it goes to VOICEMAIL in just two rings when you know that it usually takes six rings. This means that your spouse has *manually* sent you to VOICEMAIL. Depending on the phone, this is done by simply hitting the **END** key. They do this to stop the phone from ringing as they have no intention of answering your call. It is important to **note the date and time** of this because it may provide additional information later.

If you are manually sent to VOICEMAIL, it may be that your spouse is in a meeting or it may be that they are with their friend. It is only meant to provide you with additional information that, while it is not relevant now, may be in the future — so make sure to record it.

Cell Phone Technology

Now is the time to talk about the internal components of cell phones. Remember what I said earlier: *The level of success will always be proportionate to the level of knowledge you have on a specific topic.* Don't get tempted to jump to the next topic, stay the course. Learning the information will make you feel more confident about your activities and you will stun and amaze people when you start to use terms such as CDMA, TDMA, GSM, and flash memory . . . especially when you truly understand cell phone technologies.

Cell phones have a great deal of complexity built into a small housing, which enables users to store contact information, track daily tasks, manage appointments, perform numeric calculations, send and receive e-mail, send and receive text-messages, take pictures, view streaming video, obtain streaming information such as news and stock quotes, play games, play music, and then integrate all these features by synchronizing the data to their desktop computer. Wow! What a powerful, feature-rich device. Yet all of this is made possible by less then ten components that are installed into one housing. These components include a circuit board (brains of the phone), antenna, display (LCD), keyboard, speaker, battery, and a flash memory card that is attached to the circuit board and, in newer devices, a SIM card.

The circuit board controls all the input and output between the other components, as well as manages communication between the cell phone and the provider network. The antenna provides reception for the cell phone and enables a better signal from the closest cell tower. Not all cell phones have visible antennas but they are there, most likely built into the housing of the phone.

The display enables you to see data on the screen such as **Incoming calls, Outgoing numbers dialed, Text-messages, Pictures,** and so much more. The keyboard is typically located on the front of the cell phone and enables the user to input data into the phone, such as dialing numbers, creating or responding to text-messages, or e-mail. The speaker enables the user to hear ring tones, music, and a caller's voice when they call your cell phone. The battery stores the necessary voltage to make the phone work without a plug for as long as forty-eight hours, depending on the phone you have and the features that are enabled.

The only two parts that are left are the flash memory card and the SIM card. While all cell phones have flash memory cards, not all cell phones have SIM cards. This is where we start to talk about CDMA/TDMA cell phones and GSM cell phones. I am not going to get too technical and will keep it very basic in order to make it easier to understand.

TDMA stands for Time Division Multiple Access, and CDMA stands for Code Division Multiple Access. Both are commonly referred to as 2G Technology (SecondGeneration Technology). However, the only thing you have to know is that each is a way to transmit data. That's all. Not too bad. Right? So your cell phone uses either TDMA or CDMA to transmit information. CDMA/TDMA technologies have been used on many analog cellular phone systems. CDMA/TDMA phones have flash memory cards only. This is where the data you are looking for is stored.

GSM is an acronym which means Global System for Mobile communication. This is the latest cell phone technology that many providers are migrating to. The GSM technology is huge in Europe and is growing throughout the United States. Unlike other cellular systems that are analog, GSM systems are digital and communicate with cell phones that also are digital. The digital GSM cell phones have both flash memory cards *and* SIM (Subscriber Identity Module) cards. All of this is just for your knowledge and has no bearing on whether or not you can get to the data.

According to Bill Teel, President of Crownhill USA, the older phones which are still in existence, account for about 65 percent of cell phones today and have the flash memory cards that store the data. Crownhill is the producer of SIMIS, a popular SIM card interrogation software used by many law enforcement officials around the world. It was created in the United Kingdom, where, like all of Europe, the SIM card is ubiquitous.

SIMIS was the first true forensic SIM card interrogation tool, and has been referenced in many court proceedings. Teel sees the SIM's roll in investigations as limited, but necessary when he states, "While more of the phone's data is now being stored on the device, as opposed to the SIM, the SIM card should be analyzed in any investigation. The text-messages and last numbers dialed, for example, that may be left on the SIM could be extremely helpful in investigations."

If your spouse has a GSM cell phone, some data may be stored on the flash memory card and some may be stored on the SIM card. SIM is a smart card inside of a GSM cellular phone that is responsible for encrypting voice and data transmissions and stores data about the user so that they can be identified and authenticated to the provider network. The SIM also stores data such as personal phone settings and phone numbers.

The only other type of storage device that could exist on a cell phone was not manufactured with the phone. This is called an SD card, which stands for Secure Digital card. It is used to store data and move data from cell phones to other media and has many other functions as well. You can identify this easily because it is typically visible from the exterior of the cell phone and with just a little push in and release, the SD card pops back out toward you, and it can be removed from the cell phone. If the cell phone has an SD card, then it needs to be removed from the cell phone in order to get the data off the SD card.

If you have an SD card, all you have to do is go to your favorite computer store and purchase a very inexpensive SD reader and attach it to your computer. Once you do this, the computer will recognize the card as a drive and you can then use the computer forensic software to image and search the card. Please refer back to the chapter regarding analyzing computers for more information.

There are no real standards that all cell phone manufacturers follow regarding what is stored where and it is all determined by each manufacturer. This is one of the major reasons that cell phone forensics is the most difficult; and while some software products work well for getting access to data on cell phones, they don't always work well on all cell phones. So the best way to start is to know the make and model of your spouse's cell phone and contact the software publisher to find out how well it works with that phone.

When you purchase any product, make sure that you are purchasing everything you need. For example, in order to use cell phone forensic software or sync software for a particular cell phone, you will also need a data cable to connect to your computer. These data cables have two types of connections – one is a serial connection and the other is a USB connection. I would suggest getting the one with the USB connection, as most computers have a USB port to connect the cable to. The newer computers no longer provide a serial port to connect to; but if you have a computer that is at least two years old, then chances are you have a serial port, which is also commonly referred to as a COM port. This is a small connector in the rear of the computer that has nine pins that stick out. The serial port has five pins on top and four pins on the bottom and should be easy to locate. Remember you are looking for a connector that has pins that stick out, not a connector that has small pinhole sockets.

I have chosen to use the Paraben Cell Seizure™ Kit in order to walk you through the cell phone acquisition and analysis process, but you must check with the Paraben Corporation before purchasing any product to make sure it will work well for the cell phone you have. Although I use the Paraben product as a demonstration in my book, I will provide you with several other names and websites to check out their products as well. Please do your homework and you will be successful and be able to reduce your costs.

Cell phone forensics is relatively new, and the technology has not yet evolved like it has with computer forensics. Today, almost every software product that I am familiar with or have used has it limitations and/or problems. So make sure you do your homework if you plan to use a software utility to access and store data located on cell phones. Any software utility can save you time when you need to access, store, search, and retrieve data, as long as it is easy to use and does its job well. If you are not able to find such a product, then the manual method may be the best for now. I do recommend you at least try software because I believe that you will find something that will work for you.

Sync Software for Cell Phones

Cell phones can store an enormous amount as well as a variety of information – some important, and other information not as important.

Industry innovators saw a market demand for a technology that not only archived data to protect it, but also provided a host of other features to assist cell phone users. As most of you can attest, working on a cell phone to type appointments, send an e-mail, or enter a new contact can be tedious and time-consuming. It would be much easier for most of us if we had the ability to type the data into our computer and then transfer that data to the cell phone.

This is exactly the concept of sync software, which is short for synchronization software. The term *synchronization* means to synchronize the data between these two devices, which means the data transfer is two-way. New information from the phone is transferred to the computer and new information located on the computer is transferred to the cell phone.

Sync software has been used in the past by individuals who were looking into the activities of their spouse. They simply connected their spouse's cell phone to their computer, where the sync software was already installed, and selected the **Synchronize** option. All of the data from the phone came rushing onto their computer, but some people forgot that all of the data from their computer installation went rushing onto the cell phone. When their spouse found the new entries, some knew exactly what had happened, while others remained confused.

Sync software has been referred to as the poor person's forensic tool, but it really has nothing to do with forensics. If you are not interested in following an expert's methodology and you just want access to limited information, then this may be a viable solution for you. There are some limitations with the sync software, so you have to do your research. The typical sync software product will sync contact information, appointment information, photos, and e-mail messages. Now don't get too excited about the e-mail messages because you can get them from the computer anyway.

I am not familiar with any sync software products that sync the phone logs or text-messages, and this is typically what you want to get access to. This is why you need access to a hybrid sync / forensic tool or simply a forensic tool in order to access, image, locate, and retrieve the information from cell phones. My recommendation is to stay away from sync software, but I wanted to touch on it so you know all the issues. I felt that if I did not discuss the topic you might have taken that route.

Cell Phone Software Products

The cell phone forensic industry is relatively new, and there are some really neat products that have emerged. Some products work for some phones, but do not work for others. One nice application is called MOBILedit. The product is published by Compelson Laboratories and additional information can be found at www. mobiledit.com. One of the nicest options is that the company offers the product in both sync and forensic software versions. The product synchronizes all data located in the phone book, call register, calendar, to-do lists, SMS and MMS messages, and so much more. Certain features, though, are only available for certain phones based on the phone's manufacturer and model.

While I would recommend the forensic version, that decision is going to be up to you after you do some research. Remember that the forensic version is going to ensure that you don't leave telltale signs on your spouse's cell phone. The most important thing is to check MOBILedit's website to make sure that your spouse's phone is supported. If you are in doubt, send MOBILedit an e-mail to find out. By the way, you are the customer so don't be afraid to ask questions. Please make sure that you are getting everything you need, including a cable.

Oxygen Phone Manager is another really nice product that offers a sync software version. The product synchronizes all data located in the phonebook, call register, calendar, to-do lists, SMS and MMS messages, and so much more. Certain features, though, are only available for certain phones based on the phone's manufacturer and model.

Forensic Process for Cell Phones

While I hope you are reading every chapter of this book in the order that I wrote it, I also have to make the assumption that some of you may not be, so I am going to reiterate the following: *Just because you have the knowledge to perform cell phone forensics does not mean you have the legal right to do so.* Performing cell phone forensics on a device which you own or consider a marital asset should be fine, but always check with your lawyer to be sure because the law varies from state to state. If I taught you how to pick a lock, that would not give you the authority to walk into your neighbor's house, so please make sure that your activities remain within the confines of the law that is specific for your jurisdiction.

If you are performing cell phone forensics on the cell phone of a boyfriend or girlfriend, then you may be in violation of the law and subject to criminal prosecution. Again, check with your lawyer because there may be extenuating circumstances which I am not aware of, where your attorney may advise you that there is no problem. Never assume that you have the legal right, always check with your attorney. If you do not have an attorney, then find one and consult with them.

The data you are looking for is stored on either a flash memory card, SIM card, or SD (Secure Digital) card. These are known as active media, which means they have the ability to store the information even though there is no power. This means that the battery power can be completely depleted and the media will still continue to store the data forever, as long the device is not damaged. These media types can store and erase data in large blocks, making them a suitable technology for applications that frequently need to update large amounts of data, as in the case of cell phone synchronization.

If you have been reading this book in the correct order, then you should be very familiar with the principles of data protection and recovery of a hard drive located in a computer system. Media is media and flash memory is really no different than a hard drive when it comes to how data could be potentially destroyed. Deleted data on a hard drive can be permanently destroyed if we allowed new data to be placed on that same media. Well, the same thing could happen to cell phone media.

While computers can be disconnected from the Internet to prevent new data from being downloaded from the network onto the hard drive, cell phones are a little different. Cell phones are always connected to the network provider and as new cell phone calls, streaming news and stock quotes, and new text-messages are received, they all automatically bring new data onto the cell phone's storage media, causing deleted data to be permanently overwritten and destroyed. The data that gets overwritten may be one of the most important pieces of information that you may need and you will never know it.

So how do we turn **ON** the cell phone and prevent data from being received by new cell phone transactions? A few years ago, the only precaution you could have taken was to perform the cell phone forensic acquisition in an area that you knew there was absolutely no cell phone coverage. Today, you can perform this process anywhere you want thanks to a clever little bag known as a Faraday bag. This bag is designed with metal mesh that prevents signals from entering or exiting the bag. The cell phone is placed in the bag and this will prevent data from being received by the phone.

I think this is a good time to point out that you should never turn off a cell phone unless you are sure that there is no PIN (Personal Identification Number) required for the phone to boot. All phones offer a feature that allows a cell phone to boot only when a PIN has been entered. In other words, a password is required. If you are unsure, then don't turn off the cell phone or you might not be able to perform a data acquisition. There is a way around this but the storage cards (flash memory and SIM card) have to be removed and placed into a media reader, making your job a lot harder and more time-consuming. Don't take the chance.

Now for the subject of data acquisition of the cell phone. It sounds impressive when you say data acquisition and it certainly sounds complicated. Remember, my job is to take the complicated and turn it into easy-to-understand concepts, so don't worry. I want you to start using the correct terminology so you sound as impressive as possible. The process of data acquisition creates an *exact copy* of the storage media. Typically, a forensic technician will use a software product to initiate a bit stream image of the storage media and store the data to a single file on the forensic computer.

The forensic computer can be any computer, including a personal computer or laptop computer that you have. However, there are two important factors that you should consider. *Never do any work on a computer owned by you and your spouse.* They may discover that you have turned it into a forensic computer and things will never be the same, not to mention your home computer and their cell phone may disappear before you get the chance to acquire the data image. Second: *You never ever want to do any work on a computer that you will be performing a forensic acquisition on.* If you load anything on that computer, it will start to overwrite the deleted areas of the hard drive.

Once the data acquisition image has been stored on a computer, you can put the cell phone back in its place because you no longer need it. The ACQUISITION file has the entire contents of the cell phone storage media and searching it is the same as searching the cell phone itself. That means you can quickly do the acquisition and then take your time performing the analysis. Compared to a data acquisition of a hard drive, cell phone acquisitions are very fast and have the potential to provide you with an enormous amount of information.

Forensic Acquisition Software

There are many types of cell phone acquisition software products on the market and some are better than others. However, the most feature-rich and effective products can range in prices between $3,000.00 to $10,000.00. The Paraben Corporation publishes forensic software and launched their first product in 2001 for PDA devices. It is called PDA Seizure™. Since that time, Paraben has come out with other unique tools that deal with some of the smaller devices including Cell Seizure, which is priced at less than $400.00. Paraben's tools can be extremely powerful and may pose a challenge for some novice computer users. However, a little effort in learning the forensic tool will go a long way. In addition, the company is currently working on a software product designed specifically for the novice user. This may be available just after the printing of this book.

Amber Schroader is the CEO of the Paraben Corporation and has been a long-standing member of the forensic community. Amber became involved in cell phone forensics because she saw a void in the industry and a problem that needed a solution. The efforts of the Paraben Corporation have placed the reality of cell phone forensics within reach of many police budgets and now brings that same technology to you with a more user-friendly version of their Cell Seizure product. I have chosen this product to present in my book because I believe it provides a balance among features, ease of use, and pricing, and is the best suitable solution for many novice computer users. The Paraben Corporation provides you with not only the software, but also the cable of your choice, and it is priced under $400.00. So knowing what make and model phone your spouse uses is going to be important.

If you are familiar with another product that you feel more comfortable with, then by all means use that product. I mention certain products in specific areas of my book to make it easy for you so you don't have to do the research. All of the products I mention in this book I have personally used or researched and recommend them because I believe they would give you the best results for the price and are easy to use. It is up to you, of course, to decide if it will work for you. I don't know what cell phone you have, so that decision rests with you once you have completed the necessary research.

Purchasing a cell phone forensic software product will save you both time and money, which will enable you to collect information quickly to make decisions faster. If you purchase Paraben's Cell Seizure, you might think that this is where we say goodbye, but that couldn't be further from the truth. I will stay with you the entire time. I will walk you through the task of installing the software and getting everything ready for a rapid cell phone acquisition. I will never let you go off and have to do the research yourself or read a technical manual to learn something yourself. The entire concept of this book is to teach you everything I can teach you to be successful in your endeavors. My goal is to leave no questions unanswered, and I will try my best to accomplish that goal.

Let's start with getting ready to purchase the software product. First, you must know the make and model of *your spouse's* current cell phone, as well as the make and model of any older cell phone they may have been using previously that you want to take a look at. Then, you need to know the make and model of *your* cell phone. If you do not have a cell phone, then enlist the help of a friend that you trust so you can use their cell phone. If the cell phones are the same make and model, then you can save some money. If they are not, then I would highly recommend that you purchase the software product with cables for all the cell phones that you want to acquire, as well as for your cell phone or your friend's cell phone.

The reason for the additional cable is to get to know the software product and to practice acquiring data from your cell phone before you attempt an acquisition of your spouse's cell phone. Do the acquisition and analysis of your cell phone several times and print reports to make sure you are comfortable with the product and process. Please don't attempt to perform the acquisition and analysis of your spouse's cell phone without practicing first. Purchase the software and hardware (cables) and let's get it installed. If you did not purchase Cell Seizure, this is where we say goodbye because it is not possible for me to list the directions for all the products on the market today and the following text will not be useful with another product.

Installing Paraben's Cell Seizure Software

1) Having purchased the Paraben Cell Phone Seizure product, take the CD out of the plastic box it is sold with and place the CD into the computer that you are using as a forensic computer. *Please do not install this software on a computer that you need to perform computer forensics on at a later date. Remember, loading software onto a computer overwrites the deleted and unallocated spaces of the hard drive, which will reduce your chances of recovering data.*

2) When you place the CD into your forensic computer, it should automatically load the **installation** software and an **Installation** screen should appear on your monitor. If it does not, then you need to navigate your way to the CD using Windows Explorer, which you learned how to use in Chapter 5. **Double-click** on **autorun.exe**, which will execute the installation software for you and the **Installation** screen will appear.

3) When the **Installation** screen is on your monitor, you will not be able to avoid the huge letters INSTALL NOW. **Click** on

INSTALL NOW you will go to another screen that says **Welcome to Paraben's Cell Seizure** installation.

4) If you look at the bottom of the screen, you will see that **Next** is already highlighted, so all you need to do here is hit **ENTER** or **Click** on **Next.**

5) The next screen is the **EULA,** which stands for End-User License Agreement. You will notice that *I do not accept the terms in this license agreement* is checked. You must change that by **Clicking** on the words **I accept the terms in the License Agreement.**

6) *Please make sure to read the license agreement so you under-stand what you can and cannot do with the software.* After you do that, you can then hit **ENTER** or **Click** on **Next.**

7) The next screen is the **Select installation folder** screen. It is asking you where you want the PROGRAM files installed. The default path is C:\Program Files\Paraben Corporation\Cell Seizure\. I recommend that you keep the **Default** path by hitting **ENTER** or by **Clicking** on **Next.**

8) The next screen is the **Customized setup.** The Cell Seizure software has to install supporting files that will enable the soft-ware to do what you need it to do. It is asking if you want to change the way the files are installed. I recommend that you do not change anything and accept the **Default** settings by hitting **ENTER** or **Clicking** on **Next.**

9) The next screen is also a **Customize setup** screen. However, this time it is advising you that the installation process should either install or update the drivers on your hard drive that will enable your USB cable to connect your cell phone to the computer. The software application recommends that you have the newest drivers installed or updated. You can accom-plish this by **Clicking in the little square white box.** This will place a check mark in that box.

10) You can then hit **ENTER** or **Click Next.**

11) The next screen is the **Ready to install** screen. It is a screen that is advising you that when you **Click** on the **Install** button, the product will be installed on your computer. The only thing left to do is to **Click** on the **Install** button and the **Installing Paraben's Cell Seizure** screen will appear with a STATUS BAR that will show you the progress of the installation. In a very short time, you will see a black box appear on the screen, just ignore this. It is the application doing what it is supposed to be doing.

11) Then you may get a box that says **Digital signature not found.** This is a standard message you sometimes get when you install a product that was not made or tested by the Microsoft Corporation. Just **Click** on **Yes** and the installation process will continue.

12) The installation procedure will continue and you will then come to a screen that says **Welcome to the InstallShield wizard for PL-2303 USB-to-serial.** Remember, this is the product that I am working with at the time I am writing this book. If the installation product you are working with is a little different, don't worry. Just **Click** on **Next** to continue.

13) The next screen is the **InstallShield Wizard complete** screen. This screen is advising you that you have successfully completed the installation processes for Paraben's Cell Seizure software. All you have to do here is **Click** on **Finish.**

14) The installation screen will appear for a short time and then go to the final screen, which is the **Completing Paraben's Cell Seizure installation. Click** on **Finish** again and you are done.

15) The only thing left to do is **Click** on **Exit**, located on the bottom right side of the original screen that appeared.

Congratulations you have just installed Paraben's Cell Phone Seizure forensic software.

An important note with software products is that occasionally they use other tools from larger software publishers to make their software work. This is the case with Paraben's Cell Seizure, as it uses a tool from Microsoft called .NET. This .NET application is also included with the Cell Seizure software disks and installs very easily by following the next prompts on your computer just like the Cell Seizure installation. In the installation process, if you did not have .NET already installed, Cell Seizure would have prompted you to do so.

Starting the Cell Phone Seizure Software

1) On your **Desktop** you should see a new icon named **Cell Seizure,** which should be a reddish color. **Double-click** on that icon and the software application will start.

2) The first thing that will come up is a warning box titled **Paraben's registration reminder.** It is reminding you to register the software, but we do not have to do that right now. According to the company's documentation, you can continue to use the software application thirteen times or for thirty days, whichever comes first. After the thirteenth time you start the software application or if thirty days passes, the application will not start. So take the time when you can to register the software you purchased at the Paraben website. For now, you can **Click** on **OK** and the software application continues to start.

3) The software application brings you to a screen titled **Paraben's Cell Seizure.** There are several menu options that enable you to perform multiple tasks. Rather than go through them and have you forget something, we are just going to jump right in and start a cell phone acquisition. First off, connect the proper cable to the cell phone and then connect that cable to your PC. If you are unsure about where to connect the cable, then take a look at the end of the cable. You will notice that it will only fit one type of port on the computer, and that will be either the Serial or USB port. Plug

it into that port and make sure you don't have the cable upside down.

4) Now it is time to turn **ON** your cell phone (or your friend's cellphone).

5) If the cable is a USB cable, you will see another screen appear, advising you that it found new hardware and that again the **Digital signature not found.** Just **Click** on **Yes** and the software application will install the necessary drivers you need so the computer can communicate with the phone.

6) After you **Click** on **Yes,** the software application will do what it needs to do. This means you are ready to perform your very first cell phone acquisition.

7) On the top of the screen you will notice several menu options that move from the left to the right. Counting from the left menu option titled **File,** go to the *fifth* menu option to the right, which is titled **Tools. Click** on **Tools.**

8) The first menu option on the top is **Acquisition. Click** on the **Acquisition** menu option.

9) This will bring up a screen titled **Welcome to Paraben's Cell Seizure acquisition wizard. Click** on **Next.**

10) The next screen is the **Open/create workspace.** The software is asking you to name the file you want to save the data to and where you want to place that file on your hard drive. If you are reading this book in order, you should know how to navigate the file system using Windows Explorer and how to create a folder. The software application will walk you through creating a folder; you just have to **Click** on the **Browse** button to show the software application where you want to place that folder. Go ahead and create a folder called TCPA, which is short for Test Cell Phone Acquisition. You'll know what it means, but if someone saw it by accident, they would not know what it was.

11) The only thing left to do here is give the file a name. Let's name it TEST and then **Click** on **OK.**

12) This will bring up a small screen titled **Paraben's Cell Seizure acquisition wizard** advising you that the database **Test** does not exist. Just **Click** on **Yes** and the program will create the file for you.

13) You will see a screen titled **Cell Seizure acquisition wizard** advising you that you are creating a file called TEST and the path it will be going. You should see something like C:\tcpa\test.csz, so just **Click** on **Next.**

14) The next screen is again a **Cell Seizure acquisition wizard** screen and asks you to identify who made the phone. You can choose from a list using the pull-down menu by hitting the **Arrow** that is facing downward on the right side. Choose the manufacturer of the phone you are doing the acquisition on and **Hit Next.** The next screen is similar but this time it is asking you to choose a model. If your model appears in the list then choose it, but if it does not then choose **AutoDetect** and then **Click** on **Next.**

15) The next screen is again similar, but this time you are asked to choose the connection type — in other words, the type of cable you used to connect your cell phone to the computer. The options are USB, COM1(which means it is a serial cable or a modem). If you have been reading this book in chapter order, you should know the difference between a USB cable and a serial cable. As a reminder, the serial cable has pins at the end and the USB does not. Choose the correct cable type and then **Click** on **Next.**

16) The next screen has **Acquisition options,** which are all checked. Leave this as it is and it will acquire all of the information that is on your phone. Uncheck any of the boxes and it will not acquire the information that you unchecked.

17) The next screen is just a review of how you configured this acquisition. Take a look at it just to get an overall idea of the steps you just completed. The data on this screen should make sense to you since you just went through the configuration. After you take a quick look, **Click** on **Next.**

18) The acquisition will start; however, you may experience a problem if you do not have the latest drivers or if your phone connection is not stable. If you do encounter a problem, contact the Paraben Corporation and ask for technical support. This is the reason you need to register the product. If you are not having a problem, then the software application should go through the acquisition with no problem.

19) The cell phone acquisition should take about ten to twenty minutes to complete. The nice thing is that cell phone image files are small and can be sent out to an expert via e-mail in order to obtain the necessary data if you are unable to successfully learn all you need to learn.

Analyzing the Acquisition File

This section assumes that you were successful in imaging your spouse's cell phone and that you now have a forensic image of that cell phone on the computer that you are using as a forensic computer.

1) The first step is to start the **Paraben's Cell Seizure** application. Then along the top left corner of the screen you will see a menu option titled **File. Click** on the **File** menu option.

2) **Scroll down** and **Click** on the **Open** option.

3) This will open a window that will enable you to browse the local hard drive for the PARABEN IMAGE file. This will be the file that you named. Just to the left of the name will be a square red icon with Paraben's design on it. **Click** on this IMAGE file and the cell phone image will be loaded into the application.

4) The data will open in a Windows Explorer-like environment, which will give you the ability to **Navigate** your way though the data. There will be folders that will be labeled CALL LOGS, PHONE BOOK and SMS HISTORY – just to name a few. SMS is an acronym for Short Message Service, which is the text-messages that you want to review.

5) The application will allow you to create bookmarks and reports. Bookmarks provide the ability to save the result of a specific search. So if you searched for all files that end with .WMV, you can bookmark a full listing of these files for later review.

Remember that cell phone forensics is not an evolved technology, but rather an evolving technology. This means that what you will be viewing will appear as raw data and may not be nicely formatted like you see when you perform computer forensics.

In addition, since every phone manufacturer and phone model may store data differently, some data may be available for some phones and not for other phones. Also, some data may not be available to you at all, even though you can see it when you view it manually while you have the phone in your hand. It will all depend on the phone.

If you purchase the application, try your best to get to know it and if you have any questions, use the application's **Help** option or call Paraben's technical support section. I have worked with Paraben's technical support people, and they have solved the issues I brought to them. The technical support team also has made recommendations to the programming division – based on the calls from users to have the software application modified in order to gain access to additional cell phone data that it may not be currently retrieving for users.

– 8 –

Locating and Analyzing E-mail

Overview

This chapter will walk you through the process of locating and analyzing e-mail stored in a variety of file formats. The process will work for you whether the e-mail files are restored from a forensic image that you created, or you simply copied the e-mail files from your spouse's computer onto a small USB drive.

I am assuming that you want to work on a computer you own, and that you have consulted with your lawyer, and that – based on their legal opinion – you are able to proceed to gain access to a message file that is stored on your computer. Please make sure that your lawyer is aware that the message file you want to access is stored on a computer you own and not stored on a server outside of your control and ownership. *If you have not consulted with an attorney or you already know that you do not have a right to access this data file, then you must not proceed.*

There are many ways we communicate today – e-mail, instant-messaging, text-messaging, and calling each other on the cell phone are a few. There are also Web forums and blogs, but technologies like these are outside of the scope of this chapter.

I am sure you have heard that instant-messaging is a fast-growing technology and that more and more people are using this type of technology to communicate. While, adolescents make up the majority of the population using this technology, that is not to say that adults don't use it. There are also specific reasons that spouses who are cheating do not use instant-messaging as much as e-mail. Instant-messaging technology is not as useful for individuals involved in cheating on their spouse because a person has to be live online to use the technology. Many individuals involved in cheating have responsibilities to attend to during the day and are often not available to chat online. In addition, people who already know each other are more likely to use instant-messaging technology to communicate with each other rather than with someone they do not know. Very few people feel comfortable chatting back and forth outside of a formal Web forum with individuals they have never met. Remember, we are not talking about chatting in a Web forum; we are talking about instant-messaging, which is more personal. So, in the world of infidelity, e-mail is the preferred method to communicate, at least until they get to know the person better.

The main reason that e-mail is the preferred method to communicate is because e-mail accounts can be set up automatically without any identifying information being attributed to that account. When you sign up for an account using a major service provider like AOL, you often have to provide a credit card and a physical street address. There are, however, literally hundreds of free Web portals where you can set up an anonymous e-mail account that can never be traced back to you if you know what you are doing.

When someone is involved in cheating on their spouse, they want to be cautious not to get caught. They don't want to interact in real-time, using a service where they can be traced, with someone that may be their spouse working undercover, a private investigator hired by their spouse, or even an undercover news reporter doing a story on cheating spouses. There is nothing worse than ending up on the front page of your local paper on Sunday morning.

Web-based e-mail accounts can also be accessed from anywhere at any time, including the person's cell phone if they have a Web-enabled phone, or at least their workplace. Even when employers monitor employees' Web activity, a visit to Yahoo.com would not raise a flag.

As you can see, cheaters like e-mail for many reasons. If your spouse is involved in cheating on you, they are most likely using e-mail to support and further their extramarital activities. The only thing you now need to determine is what type of e-mail or what e-mail client they are using.

Today, there are many of types of technologies to accomplish relatively the same objective and the different technologies have their own strengths and weaknesses. In order to help you better understand these technologies, I will review the most common types that we have found in the forensic cases I have been involved in.

It may at first start to sound complicated, but it is not. Stay the course and you will learn a lot about e-mail. Don't be tempted to give up. There is a lot to learn, but you can reduce the load by focusing on exactly what type of e-mail you will be working with. So if you know your spouse uses Outlook Express, then there is no reason to read about Outlook (a different product than Outlook Express) or American Online e-mail, and vice versa. You should at least look at all of the installed applications to be sure what your spouse is using and what they are not. For example, you may know that they use Microsoft's Outlook Express, but you may see AOL 9.0 installed on the computer. I would then take it to the next step by checking for AOL mail, just to be sure.

Web-based Mail Services

The most common type of e-mail that we find in cases of infidelity is Web-based e-mail services. Web-based e-mail is offered by major Web portals such as Yahoo!, Google, and MSN – just to name a few. You should be able to tell which service by looking at the Web history, favorites, and Web cache for your spouse's profile.

If you go to the **YAHOO! mail** login screen, you will see a yellow graphic that says **Sign up for YAHOO!** If you see this graphic in their Web cache, chances are they may have an e-mail account at Yahoo!. This is the same for Google and MSN; you have to be familiar with some of the top Web portals to make sense of what you are seeing in Web cache.

The next logical question is, *How does Web-based e-mail work?* In most cases, all the e-mail that is sent and received using one of these accounts is stored on the server that belongs to the service provider. In other words, it is not on your spouse's computer because they view their e-mail using a Web browser like Internet Explorer. However, if you are imaging the hard drive, then remnants of the messages can often be recovered since the messages were once cached on the hard drive because they were being viewed through a Web browser. The cached remnants will remain there until they are overwritten.

If you are simply copying and reviewing your spouse's PROFILE folder, then the messages will not be there, unless your spouse has paid a fee to upgrade their e-mail to POP3. POP3 technology allows us to send and receive messages from an e-mail client such as Outlook, Outlook Express, or Eudora. This means that the e-mail would then be stored on the computer your spouse uses instead of the provider's server. I can tell you from my experience spouses rarely do this because they have to use their credit card to pay for the increased service and that would affect their anonymity. That's not to say your spouse doesn't have the upgrade, it just means that most don't. This is why you have to check everything and never assume anything.

There are many issues with Web-based e-mail. *First, as a professional I have to tell you to always abide by the law – and I am serious about that.* I can also tell you that there are plenty of gray areas here. If your spouse obtained an e-mail account under false pretenses using fictitious information, are you violating their privacy when they themselves violated the policy of the Web portal, and most likely the law, themselves?

If they don't use their real name, how are you supposed to know that the account belongs to your spouse? Do you have a right, if not an obligation, to make sure who is using a fictitious account from your computer? This is why you need write down these issues and bring them to the attention of your lawyer.

I know of cases where an individual has obtained the usernames and passwords for their spouse's online accounts, has printed out the messages, and – in some cases – has changed their spouses profile to make them, let's just say, unattractive to the opposite sex. Sure I laughed when I saw what they wrote. I don't know if that activity was legal or not, but I can tell you that most lawyers probably would not be able to tell you either. My personal opinion is that it was justified and I have to believe that it made them feel better. This is a new area for lawyers, judges, and our judicial system. *Keep your lawyer up to date and never do anything without their approval.* Make sure you always stay within the bounds of the law by checking with your lawyer. In my opinion, there is nothing ever wrong with walking up to the line of what is legal, but you must *never* cross that line.

There are plenty of products on the market today that will help you recover usernames and passwords used to enter Web portals that are cached not only on the hard drive of computer systems but embedded deep into the registry of the operating system. One of the products is Registry Viewer,™ by Access Data, which will be covered in Chapter 9, Tools and Resources.

POP3 Mail Services

This section is about the POP3 protocol, another geeky way of explaining that e-mail is sent and received by an e-mail application that is installed on your computer. This is often referred to as a client application because that application is a client to the server software that actually sends and receives the mail to and from you.

POP3 is an acronym for Post Office Protocol, a set of rules used to send and receive e-mail. If a client computer used one set of rules and the server used another set of rules to send and receive e-mail, then it would not work. So, by identifying how applications should send and receive e-mail makes it easier to integrate with other applications and services.

There are plenty of products on the market today that follow the POP3 protocol. This section will discuss the most popular products that follow this protocol, describe how to identify the files, where to locate them on the hard drive, and then how to analyze them using software utilities designed to view the contents of these e-mail storage files.

First, let's see how the POP3 protocol works and how e-mail travels.

1) For the purposes of this discussion, I set up an e-mail at Yahoo!: cyberliesauthor@yahoo.com.

2) Let's also assume that both you and I were using POP3 client applications, which might be Microsoft's Outlook Express.

3) If you were to send an e-mail to cyberliesauthor@yahoo.com from your account (an example might be: youraccount@ anymailserver.com), that e-mail would be created using your POP3 e-mail client.

4) When you were done authoring the message, you would simply **Click** on the **Send** button.

5) That message is then placed in your **Outbox** and an attempt to communicate with your e-mail server (anymailserver.com) would be initiated.

6) Once a link is established to that e-mail server, the e-mail you authored is sent to the anymailserver.com server and a copy of that e-mail is then moved from your **Outbox** to your **Sent** box.

7) Now that the anymailserver.com server has the e-mail, it sends it across the Internet to the Yahoo.com server.

8) I can then login using a Web-based account to **View** and **Respond** to your message, or I could use my own e-mail client application to download it and review it on my system.

9) If I chose to use my e-mail client, all I would have to do is **Start** the application and **Click** on the **Send/receive** button. This would cause my client application to reach out to the yahoo.com server and check to see if I had any new e-mail. It would see that I had e-mail from the anymailserver.com site and transfer that e-mail from the yahoo.com server to the **Inbox** of my mail client.

These mail clients store all of the e-mail messages in different file formats based on the application that is being used. For example, Microsoft stores files in the .PST format and .DBX format, which are named as follows: CYBERLIESAUTHOR.PST, INBOX.DBX, and SENT.DBX. Netscape Messenger stores e-mail in .SMN format and

Eudora stores their mail in .MBX format. One of the nice things about technology is that all of these mail file formats can be viewed by using just one software utility.

The .PST file format is used with Microsoft Outlook, which communicates with the Microsoft Exchange Server. This file stores all e-mail, contacts, and calendaring in one file. It is possible that your spouse may use the Exchange server solely and not have a .PST stored locally on their computer. Microsoft Outlook Express uses the .DBX format and stores data in multiple files based on whether they are in the INBOX folder, SENT folder, or DELETED folder.

If you were to copy a PROFILE folder from the DOCUMENTS AND SETTINGS folder, you would obtain all of the mail for that profile on the computer, in most cases. It is, however, possible to reconfigure a system to place the mail in another location, but I have rarely seen that, if ever.

The only thing you need to know is the location of these files so you can use a utility to view the files. When you start most of the utilities, you will be asked where the specific e-mail files are located, while a few of the utilities will automatically detect the file location and instantly show you messages in the left window pane of the application. I do want to caution you when you use the utilities that automatically locate the e-mail files. *Make sure you are not looking at the e-mail files that are installed on your forensics machine and that you are actually viewing the files you stored on the external USB drive.*

That being said, all you have to do is **Highlight** one of the files in the left window pane and all the e-mail in that file will be displayed in a larger window pane on the right side. I will first review the location of each of these file types and then discuss a little about each of the applications that help you view the different e-mail formats.

Locating DBX Files

1) **Double-click** on the DOCUMENTS AND SETTINGS folder, which will list all the contents of the folder.

2) Look for the PROFILE folder that your spouse uses. **Double-click** on that folder, which will list the contents of the folder.

3) Then find the folder titled LOCAL SETTINGS, **Double-click** on that folder, and you will see the contents of the folder. If you do not see the LOCAL SETTINGS folder, then refer to option 6 on page 88 for review.

4) Look for the folder titled APPLICATION DATA and **Double-click** on that folder, which will list the contents of that folder.

5) Find the folder titled IDENTITIES and **Double-click** on that folder. You will see the contents of that folder.

6) You may see one or more folders that have numbers and letters as the folder name. You may have to **Check** each one, but let's start with the top one listed. **Double-click** on that folder, which will list the contents of the folder.

7) Locate a folder titled MICROSOFT and **Double-click** on that folder, which will list the contents of the folder.

8) Now find a folder titled OUTLOOK EXPRESS and **Double-click** on that folder, which will list all the e-mail files you are looking for.

It sounds like a lot, but you can get to these files in literally seconds. The full file path for these folders is E:\Documents and Settings\UserProfile\Local_Settings\Application_Data\Identities\ 79ABF54-924B-4D67-9621-A9987ECW4U43\Microsoft\Outlook Express\ . . . all your e-mail files. The path you see will be slightly different, as your drive might be different. The profile name will be different and the folder name that consists of numbers and letters will be different. Take your time and you will easily find them.

If all else fails, just do a search using the Microsoft search utility that you learned in the Windows File system chapter to search for *.DBX and you will find where they are. You could also use the other product that finds them for you automatically.

One last note: As I use examples, I often refer to full file paths starting with C:\ – however, if your system is configured with the DOCUMENTS AND SETTINGS folder or the PROGRAM FILES folder installed on the (**D:**) drive, then you must substitute the **C:** with **D:**. This will most likely not be the case for most of you, but I thought it necessary to point that out. It will be more obvious what I am talking about as you continue to read.

Locating PST Files

1) **Double-click** on the DOCUMENTS AND SETTINGS folder, which will list all the contents of that folder.

2) Look for the PROFILE folder that your spouse uses and then **Double-click** on that folder. You will now see a list of the contents of the folder.

3) Find the folder titled LOCAL SETTINGS and **Double-click** on that folder, which will list the contents of that folder. If you do not see the LOCAL SETTINGS folder, then refer to option 6 on page 88 for review.

4) Now, look for the folder titled APPLICATION DATA. **Double-click** on that folder. The contents of the folder will now appear.

5) Locate a folder titled MICROSOFT and **Double-click** on that folder, which will list the contents of that folder.

6) Find a folder titled OUTLOOK and **Double-click** on that folder. You will see a list of all the .PST files that you are looking for. The full file path for the .PST file is C:\Documents and Settings\UserProfile\LocalSettings\ApplicationData\Microsoft\Outlook\.

If all else fails, just do a search using the Microsoft search utility that you learned in the Windows File system chapter to search for *.PST and you will find where they are. Remember, there is a possibility that your spouse may not have the system configured to have a .PST on the computer.

Locating SNM Files

1) **Double-click** on the DOCUMENTS AND SETTINGS folder, which will list all the contents of that folder.

2) Next, look for the PROFILE folder that your spouse uses and **Double-click** on that folder. You will now see a list of the contents of that folder.

3) Find the folder titled LOCAL SETTINGS. **Double-click** on that folder, which will list the contents of that folder. If you do not see the LOCAL SETTINGS folder, then refer to option 6 on page 88 for review.

4) Now look for the folder titled APPLICATION DATA and **Double-click** on that folder. A list showing the contents of the folder will be displayed.

5) Then look for a folder titled MOZILLA and **Double-click** on that folder, which will list the contents of that folder.

6) Find a folder titled NS4DATA and **Double-click** on that folder, and you will see a list of the contents of the folder.

7) Then **Click** on the folder bearing the USERNAME that your spouse is using on Netscape and **Click** on the folder titled MAIL. The full file path is C:\DocumentsandSettings\user_name\ApplicationData\Mozilla\Profiles\ns4data\user_name\mail.

If all else fails, just do a search using the Microsoft search utility that you learned in the Windows File system chapter to search for *.SNM and you will find where they are.

Locating MBX Files

1) **Double-click** on the DOCUMENTS AND SETTINGS folder, which will list all the contents of that folder.

2) Find the PROFILE folder that your spouse uses and **Double-click** on that folder. You will see the contents of the folder.

3) Then look for the folder titled APPLICATION DATA. **Double-click** on that folder, which will list the contents of the folder.

4) Next, find a folder titled QUALCOMM and **Double-click** on that folder. The contents of the folder will be displayed.

5) Now look for a folder titled EUDORA and **Double-click** on that folder, which will contain the e-mail files. The full file path is C:\Documents and Settings\UserProfile\Application Data\ Qualcomm\Eudora.

If all else fails, just do a search using the Microsoft search utility that you learned in the Windows File system chapter to search for *.MBX and you will find where they are.

E-mail File Viewers

The first product that I am going to mention is DBXanalyzer™, a great product to search and view .DBX files and rapidly review the messages contained in each file. The application can be downloaded from www.di-mgt.com/dbxanalyzer.

The second product is Accurate Outlook Express Mail Expert™. This is the product that will automatically locate all the .DBX files on your system and even repair them if they are damaged. The application can be downloaded from www.AccurateSolution.net.

The third product is Mail Navigator™, a powerful utility that will help you review the contents of e-mail files rapidly. The application can be downloaded from www.MailNavigator.com

DBXanalyzer is available as a free download and it has a ten-day trial period where you can use it without payment. I would highly recommend that you take advantage of the ten-day grace period and make sure you like it before you purchase it. You also might get all your work done before the end of the ten-day period, so you may just save some money.

1) Whether you downloaded it for free or you end up purchasing the DBXanalyzer, **Install** the product.

2) Once the installation is complete, **Start** the application. It is an easy installation process so there is absolutely no need to go through it with you.

3) After the download, there should be a box that gives you the option to **Open, Open folder,** or **Close. Choose** the **Open** option and follow the prompts. All you have to do is basically keep **Clicking** on **Next.**

4) When the application is started, go to the top left side of the **Application** window and **Click** on **File.**

5) Then choose the first option, **Open DBX File.**

6) This will bring up a new window titled **Open.** Toward the top there will be the words **Look in:** followed by an empty text box. Just to the right of that text box should be a **Pull-down** option with a graphic image of an **Arrow** pointing down. **Click** on the **Arrow** that is pointing down.

7) This will let you select a hard drive, so **Choose** the external USB drive where you have stored the DOCUMENTS AND SETTINGS folder and navigate your way to the folder containing the .DBX files you want to review. It's that easy.

Accurate Outlook Mail Expert is available as a free download and it has a limited trial period where you can use it without payment. Additional information can be obtained from their website. I would highly recommend that you take advantage of the trial period and make sure you like it before you purchase it. You also might get all your work done before the trial period ends, so you may just save some money.

1) Whether you downloaded it for free or you end up purchasing Accurate Outlook Mail Expert, **Install** the product.

2) Once the installation is complete, **Start** the application. It is an easy installation process so there is absolutely no need to go through it with you.

3) After the download, there should be a box that gives you the option to **Open, Open folder,** or **Close. Choose** the **Open** option and just follow the prompts. All you have to do is basically keep **Clicking** on **Next.**

4) When the application is started, it automatically locates and displays all the mail folders. However, make sure that they are not the mail folders from your forensics machine that you are working on. In order to be sure, go to the top left side of the screen and **Click** on **File,** then **Scroll down** to the first option, **Open DBX File.**

5) Once you **Click** on this option, a window will open letting you **Browse** to your external USB drive.

6) By now, you should know the path (where the files are stored) to the .DBX files located on your external USB drive. All you have to do is simply **Click** on one of .DBX files and the file will open. You will be able to review and search all of the e-mail located in that file. However, you will have to open each file individually using this method. I would therefore recommend starting with the INBOX.DBX file, and then working to the SENT.DBX file, and then on to the remaining files.

Mail Navigator is available as a free download and it has a limited trial period where you can use it without payment. Additional information can be obtained from their website. I would recommend that you take advantage of the trial period and make sure you like it before you purchase it. You also might get all your work done before the trial period ends so you may just save some money.

1) Whether you downloaded it for free or you ended up purchasing Mail Navigator; **Install** the product.

2) Once the installation is complete, **Start** the application. It is an easy installation process so there is absolutely no need to go through it with you.

3) After the download, there should be a box there that gives you the option to **Open, Open folder,** or **Close. Choose** the **Open option** and follow the prompts. All you have to do is basically keep **Clicking** on **Next.**

4) Once you have the application installed, **Start** it by **Double-clicking** the appropriate icon.

5) Next, go to the top left side of the screen and **Click** on **File. Scroll down** to the **Load external mailbox** option.

6) Once you **Click** on this option, a window opens letting you **Browse** to your external USB drive.

7) By now, you should know the path (where the files are stored) to the e-mail files are located on your external USB drive. All you have to do is simply **Click** on one of the e-mail files and it will open the file and you will be able to review and search all of the e-mail located in that file.

All the applications that I briefly discussed provide instant access to e-mail files and have very powerful searching features that will enable you to find what you need very quickly. I would recommend that you take the time to download and install all of them in order to decide which application will work best for you and fit your needs. Once you decide which product to purchase, I also recommend that you take the time to get to know the application and learn about all the features so you can be as productive and efficient as possible.

AOL E-mail

AOL is one of the leading providers of online services in the world today and offers e-mail and instant-messaging, which are just two of the many services they provide. An AOL account will enable the user to set up as many as seven screen names. While AOL e-mail is often stored on the

AOL servers, America Online enables users to store e-mail on the user's local hard dive in an AOL proprietary format known as a PERSONAL FILING CABINET (.PFC). In addition to e-mail, the PERSONAL FILING CABINET can store newsgroup messages, downloaded files, favorite places, the user's address book, and much more.

The AOL PERSONAL FILING CABINET can be configured on the user's local hard drive, if the user selects this option during the installation of the AOL software. However, I have found through my experience that whether it is done accidentally or purposely, PERSONAL FILING CABINETS are created on the local drive more often than not. This means that you have a very good chance of retrieving e-mail from the .PFC file if, in fact, your spouse is using AOL.

AOL has been around for many years, so the main issue that you may face is which version of AOL your spouse is using. AOL is currently at version 9.0; but there are many individuals who are still using versions 8.0 and 7.0, as well as much older versions. For the purposes of this book, we will discuss versions 6.0 through 9.0. The only difference among these versions for our purposes is the location of the PERSONAL FILING CABINET files, which store most of the data you want to access. Once you know where to get the files from, the process is the same for all versions.

I will review a little about the AOL files that were installed if your spouse uses AOL. In AOL version 9.0, the APPLICATION files and some data files were installed in a folder titled AOL 9.0, which is located in the PROGRAM FILES directory. The full file path is C:\Program Files\AOL 9.0. The user data is installed in a folder titled ORGANIZE, which is located under the DOCUMENTS AND SETTINGS folder. The full file path is C:\Documents and Settings\All Users\Application Data\AOL\America Online 9.0\Organize. So if your spouse is using AOL 9.0, when you **Copy** this folder located in the DOCUMENTS AND SETTINGS folder you will be getting the AOL mail files also.

In AOL version 8.0 and version 7.0, the .PFC file is not stored in the DOCUMENTS AND SETTINGS folder at all. The .PFC file is stored in the ORGANIZE folder that is located in the AMERICA ONLINE 8.0 folder, which is stored the PROGRAM FILES folder. The full file path for this is

C:\Program Files\America Online 8.0\Organize. If you know your spouse is using AOL 8.0, then you must copy this folder also if you want to get access to the mail. If, however, you imaged the drive, then you have everything already and there is no reason for concern.

In AOL version 6.0 the .PFC file is not stored in the DOCUMENTS AND SETTINGS folder. The .PFC file is stored in the ORGANIZE folder, which is stored in the AMERICA ONLINE 6.0 folder, which is located in the root of drive (C:). The full file path is C:\America Online 6.0\Organize.

If you are using the FTK Imager product or Windows Explorer, you can view the contents of the ORGANIZE folder. In this folder, you will see approximately six files. All of the files should be named after the screen names that have been set up. Let's assume for the purposes of this exercise that your spouse's screen name was JSMITH. You would see the following files that were created when your spouse created that screen name: JSMITH, JSMITH.ABI, JSMIT.ABY, JSMITHL.ARL, JSMITH.AUT, and JSMITH.BAG. The one file that is most important to you is the first file that does *not* have a file extension. This is the file that contains the PERSONAL FILING CABINET and contains most of what you need.

1) The first step is to use your forensics machine and **Install** the newest version of AOL. You can obtain a copy from most places that rent videos or even a major retail outlet will have them on the counter as free giveaways. In order to be safe and avoid an accidental login attempt to an account you do not own, I would also make sure that the computer you are using is kept offline. *If you have an Internet connection, disconnect it now.* Remember, *never install AOL on the target computer or any computer that you keep at home unless your spouse no longer lives there.* They may find it and wonder what's going on.

2) Now that the newest version of AOL is installed on your forensic computer, you need to take the file we spoke about and **Place** that in the ORGANIZE folder of your forensics machine. The full file path should be C:\Documents and

Settings\All Users\Application Data\AOL\America Online 9.0\Organize.

3) Then you need to **Rename** the file by just adding a file extension to the file name. So, if the file name is JSMITH, you need to rename the file to JSMITH.PFC. In order to rename the file, all you have to do is use Windows Explorer and navigate your way to the file. Then highlight the file and **Right-click** on it. This will bring up a menu and you then choose the **Rename** option. When you do so, it will give you the ability to rename it. For purposes of this example rename it JSMITH.PFC.

4) When this has been completed, you then **Start** the AOL application that you installed on your forensics machine. When you do, you will see a login prompt. You can simply disregard this or just **Click** on **Cancel.**

5) Then go to the top left of the screen and you should see the **File menu** option. **Click** on the **File menu** option.

6) **Scroll down** to the **Open** option, which will bring up a window that enables you to **Browse** to a file.

7) **Navigate** your way to the file that you just renamed and then **Click** on that file.

8) Now **Click OK.** This should open the file and you should be able to see all of the e-mail, attachments, and other information stored in that file.

You may find that some attachments, such as photos, are not stored on the local machine and a login to AOL is required in order to see the attachments. There is nothing I can do about that and this is where my part ends. *My advice is never to login to any account that is stored on a server outside of your control and ownership without first discussing that with your lawyer and getting their approval.*

In the event you are unable to complete these steps, there is software that will convert the AOL .PFC file into other mail formats for you to access and review. One of these applications is known as ePreserver and additional information can be found on the website http://www.connectedsw.com/Overview/57266. In addition, this product is covered in Chapter 9, Tools and Resources.

We covered a lot of information about e-mail, but don't let it overwhelm you. Focus only on what type of e-mail format your spouse is using, and that's it. Follow the simple steps and you will amaze yourself. Take the steps one at a time and you will be successful.

Tools and Resources

Overview

This book is designed to be a technical reference for you to follow in order to help you accomplish your objectives. As technology continues to rapidly advance, some of the information in this book – as it relates to tools and technologies – can become outdated. In order to continue to provide you with the most current information, the CyberLies.com website should be your main resource. For individuals who purchased this book, CyberLies.com will continue to provide the latest information to make sure you are kept up to date. This does not mean that the CyberLies.com website will *replace* this book. For instance, information such as the forensic process and methodology that you need to know will not be covered on the website. The website will continue to support the book with short training videos to assist novice computer users in understanding how to navigate the Windows file system, how to copy files from one drive to another using Windows Explorer, how to search the Windows file system to locate additional information, and other videos that we may release in the future. While some of these tasks may be easy for many readers, it can appear complex to those who do not work with these features on a regular basis. All of these, as well as our future plans for helping you, will be covered on our website.

This chapter is designed to cover the tools and resources available to help support your forensic activities. While it is not possible to cover all categories and types of products available, I have identified only a few of the products that I believe are important for you to know about because I don't want to overwhelm you with too much information. The book is packed with enough information for you to absorb already and additional products may be covered on our website after the book is released.

I also want to make it perfectly clear that I am mentioning some of these products because I believe that they may be of use to you and make your task easier. I am not receiving any commission or referral fee whatsoever from any third-party product or service identified in this book because I personally believe that this would be a conflict for me.

The two main categories of this chapter will be Services and Products. These may include websites, search utilities, and other products or services that might make it easier to help you attain your goals and objectives. It is worth taking the time to review each of the technologies discussed in this chapter to see if they are of use to you. The more you know about what is available, the more resourceful you can be.

Services

The best place to start will be with Internet-based services available for free. The most obvious to start with is your favorite search engine, which most of us take for granted. By now, you should know how these search engines get their data, so you will also know that when someone leaves their name or phone number somewhere on the Internet, these search engines will index that data for you to find.

Therefore, if you have discovered a person's name, Web forum handle, e-mail address, or phone number, you should go to your favorite search engine and perform a search on that piece of information. The search engine might return a result that you would not have expected. I entered my e-mail on Google.com and **Clicked** on **Search**. Google returned several websites that I was affiliated with or had written articles for. I then typed a portion of my address, surrounded by quotation marks, in the Google.com search engine. It returned several other sites that listed my company address. I didn't need my name or company, I just typed my street address in like this: **street address here,** and it returned the results. The quotation marks enclosing a phrase help any search engine focus on that *exact* phrase.

By searching for a person's name, you may be able to obtain additional information about the person that you would never have identified. It might be another site they are also involved in, or it might be other people they are involved with. It might also lead to nothing; but you know the saying, "nothing ventured, nothing gained."

You might be thinking that your favorite search engine may not have the data you are searching for and you should be conducting the same search using multiple search engines. Good thinking! Wouldn't it be nice if you could query multiple search engines at the same time. You can! There are multiple search engines that query a multitude of other search engines and return the search results to you. These include dogpile.com, metacrawler.com, and searchallinone.com, just to name a few. If you want a better listing, just go to your favorite search engine and type in **search multiple search engines**, and you should get a nice listing.

There are also many free services that will enable you to identify the owners of websites and IP addresses. Sites that include NetworkSolutions.com, Enom.com, and Register.com all have this data available, and you get instant access for free. Just **Click** on the **Whois** option at any one of these sites, and fill in the information that you want to look up.

Many phone search services are provided free of charge. They enable you to type in a person's name or address, and the service gives you a phone number. You can also identify a person's address by entering their name and state. You can even perform a reverse lookup, which is identifying a person by entering their phone number. So, if you find a phone number that may be important, you might be able to identify who owns the phone number. *(Refer back to page 30 for specifics.)*

These phone search services are also provided for cell phones. I would, however, caution you about some of the sites that offer these services. In some sites, you get to perform the search for free, but the companies do not provide you with the data unless you register or pay a fee. The site may say that they found similar data or traces of that data, but they will not reveal the information without payment.

I have received e-mails from people who have paid for information and received nothing. Be careful or you could be spending money needlessly. My advice to you is, *If a site tells you that it's for free and then you have to start entering your personal information or pay, walk away from that site.* There are plenty of sites that have this service available for free; you don't have to waste your time with misleading information from other sites. However, if you found a legitimate site that charges for this information and you feel it is worth the cost, then by all means purchase the information. I am only talking about leaving sites that advertise one thing and then do another.

There are resources available that help you identify flight arrivals and departures in case your spouse says they are traveling. If they tell you that they are flying on business from one state to another using their favorite airline, then you have the ability to verify this. While you may not be able to see if they actually made it to that flight, you would be able to check to see if that flight actually took off and arrived. All you need is the date and flight number. Hey, not bad information for free! One helpful site is flightarrivals.com. There are several places that offer these services. All you have to do is a search using your favorite search engine to identify these sites.

The top dating and cheating sites are also great resources for you to see if your spouse has a profile on any of these sites. The one thing working against a cheating spouse is the fact that their partner knows a lot about them. All you have to do is search these sites with criteria that would fit your spouse and you may find their profile and even a picture of them on one of these sites. Yes, sometimes they are that stupid.

Computer Products

This book has covered a lot of information and provided you a better understanding of not only technology, but also recovering data from hard drives. You may not have recovered all the data you need; and even if you have, you may not know what next steps you should take.

The first product that I would like to talk about is known as a keyboard logger or keylogger. These products, sold as both hardware and software, address both workstation computers and laptop computers. *For the purposes of this discussion, you should never load any software on a computer unless you first image the computer's hard drive.*

The purpose of a keylogger is to record the keyboard strokes of an individual using a keyboard. These products can actually store millions of keystrokes, which will enable you to retrieve USERNAMES and PASS-WORDS for not only computers, but also for websites they visit.

The hardware version of a keylogger is made for full-size computers that have a keyboard connected to it via a port in the back of the computer. This is very hard to detect because most of us never check the back of the computer. It is a small inline device that is almost never detected.

The software version of the keylogger is made for laptop computers that do not have attached keyboards. I would not suggest using this product, though, unless you have imaged that drive first. This way, you are not potentially destroying the very data you are attempting to recover.

When you use a keylogger to learn what keystrokes were entered on the computer, a special keystroke series is entered and you can then view all the data on the keylogger. It is easy to identify USERNAMES and PASSWORDS, as well as anything else that is typed – including real-time chats. However, you will only see what is typed by the keyboard and not what the responding party has typed. It is one of the most popular methods that spouses use to determine the USERNAME and PASSWORDS to the computer and or to forums at specific websites.

The next product category that is important for spouses to know about is often referred to as *snoopware*. Spyware is another word for it, but this is sometimes confused with what marketing firms load on your computer to track shopping and surfing habits. The snoopware prod-ucts can be very powerful applications that track everything that is done on that computer. Snoopware then can store the results or send alerts to you in real-time. These products are often very easy to install and can often be virtually undetectable. They will record e-mail sent and received, instant-messaging, chat sessions, websites visited, peer-to-peer file sharing, and can even take screen shots for later review.

In one case that I became aware of, a husband stayed up all night chatting with a go-go dancer online while his wife slept. Their communication went on for several hours and deteriorated into several lewd and lascivious acts, which were all very explicit. When the husband woke up the next morning, he was confronted with printouts of his online conversation and his bags were already packed and waiting for him at the door. Not a very good way to start the day!

Remember never use one of these products unless you have imaged the drive first. These products can tell you what your spouse will be up to from the date you install the product, but they can never tell you what they have been up to prior to the installation. They can, of course, destroy all of that information when they are installed and then continue to destroy that information as their files build in size. They are great products to use, but only after you image the drive.

File viewers are another category of products that you need to know about. By now, you realize that while you may have recovered data, certain file types may require a specific application to view the contents of that data file. This means you would be required to purchase and install several different applications in order to see that data. There are, however, software utilities designed to provide the ability to view multiple data types. Further, you may not need utilities at all to view other data types.

So let's start with graphic files, which include but are not limited to the following file extensions: JPG, JPEG, .BMP, .TIF, .TIFF, and .GIF. The file name can be ROBERT.JPG, MARY.TIF, or JAMIE.GIF. The one thing they all have in common is that they are graphic files. You can identify files because of their file extension. The file extension may not always be visible, but it starts just after the dot (.) in the file name and has three letters and sometimes four. The nice thing about graphic files is that most of them are viewable in Microsoft Windows Explorer and there is usually no need to purchase a graphic file viewer.

As you navigate the Windows file system using Windows Explorer, you should be able to see the files. If you are just seeing the file names, then this is what you have to do to see the pictures.

1) Note that there is a menu bar that runs along the top left of the Windows Explorer window. One of these options is **View**. Using your pointer **Click** on **View.**

2) **Scroll down** to **Thumbnails** and **Click** on that option. The nice powerful part of this utility is that if you see a folder and it has graphic files in it, that means there are pictures in that folder. If you see a folder that has no pictures in it, then you don't have to waste your time going into it if you are only interested in viewing graphic files.

Graphic files are great to review because this will tell you what type of activity your spouse may be involved in. For example, thumbnail pictures of women or men might indicate that they are on dating or cheating sites. Web cache will tell you what sites your spouse visits on a regular basis. Pictures taken with cell phones and cameras can also reveal information that is often found on the computer when these devices are synchronized with the computer.

Another popular file type is .DBX, which is a Microsoft Outlook Express mailbox. Some of these file names include INBOX.DBX, SENT.DBX, OUTBOX.DBX, and DRAFT.DBX. All of them hold mail that has either been sent, waiting to be sent, or received. You cannot just **Click** on these files and open them, though. They must be viewed with a product that knows how to read their format.

One such product is DBXanalyzer, which will instantly let you see the contents of every message in each .DBX file. This powerful application will also let you search each .DBX file based on date range, e-mail address, or any word that might appear in the message. The nice feature is that you do not need to install Microsoft Outlook Express to view the messages. Additional information about this product can be found at the website: www.di-mgt.com.au/dbxanalyzer. The site offers a free demo that can be immediately used to start viewing your spouse's e-mail that you recover.

Mail Navigator is another product that will allow you to view the contents of file types which include the file extensions of .DBX, .MDX, and .PST. (These are all different file types that are supported by one application.) Additional information about this product can be found at their website www.mailnavigator.com/read_dbx_file.html. It is important to do a little research to make sure what you need to purchase, but also to realize that most of these applications you can use for free for a short period of time. You'll want to do this before you purchase anything to make sure the software works well for you.

Explorer View is yet another application that I recommend very highly. This application will help reduce the time you spend in reviewing data, as it allows you to view a number of data formats (including the Web history) while providing an environment similar to Windows Explorer. Additional information about Explorer View can be found at www.explorerview.com. It will be well worth your time to review its powerful capabilities.

ePreserver.com provides a product that allows you to convert AOL.PFC e-mail files to Outlook or Outlook Express e-mail, if doing that makes it easier for you to review files. Additional information about ePreserver can be found at www.connectedsw.com/Overview/57266. I would check this application out very closely. If it works well for you, it may save you time.

Access Data also has a product called Registry Viewer. This software will enable you to gain access to additional information, including auto complete form data from the major search engines, Internet account USERNAMES and PASSWORDS, Outlook and Outlook Express account information, as well as a Web search terms – even if your spouse clears the cache and shreds the deleted areas of the hard drive. All of this information, stored in the registry located in a file called NTUSER.DAT, is very valuable for your research efforts. If you don't want to purchase the product and then have to learn how to access this file, we offer a low-cost service to do that for you. All you have to do is send us one file via e-mail and we will do the rest. For additional information, please feel free to contact us at (888) 674-4872.

There is one more product that I want to mention. It is outside the box in terms of computer forensics, but may help you in finding additional information. The product assists you in physically tracking your spouse's vehicle. It is a low-cost solution that enables you to place a device in the trunk of the car. Then, it records the position of the vehicle all day. When the vehicle arrives home, all you have to do is download the data into your laptop computer and then play it back on the computer using a mapping program that is sold with the application. It is amazing technology that is sold for under $300.00 and you can see the exact route and every stop made by the vehicle. I am sure there are many companies that have similar products, but the one I tested and used is made by Deluo Electronics. Additional information can be obtained from the website at www.deluoelectronics.com.

The one bit of advice that I want to leave you with is to make sure you do your homework before purchasing any product or service. There are plenty of sites that are designed to take as much of your money as they can, and being in a vulnerable state may make you a willing victim. Keep alert; and if you think for one minute that a site has misled you, then go looking for another site. There are fortunately some great sites that are genuine in their offerings.

I want you to be successful for the least amount of money expended; and if you are diligent, you may not have to spend any money to find the information you need to make decisions. That is the goal of *Cyber Lies* and it should be yours as well.

– 10 –

Organizing Your Efforts

Overview

There is no doubt that by now you have learned more than you ever knew about locating, recovering, and reviewing data stored on computer systems and cell phones. I will be the first to tell you that it is a lot of information to digest. I have been doing this for almost two decades and it was certainly a lot of information to write about.

This chapter is not about designing a plan for you; I can't. There are too many variables. So, I have decided to walk you through a process that lets you take charge and lets you decide what you want to do and how you want to accomplish it. The goal of this chapter is to help you start to think about what you need and get you to ask the right questions, so you can obtain the necessary answers before you proceed.

So, where do you begin? The best place to begin is by developing a plan that identifies your goals and objectives. To some, that may be by taking small steps, while others may decide to plunge in and get it over with. So your first main objective should be in the development of a plan that is flexible and allows you to make adjustments as you receive new information.

I want you to understand that this chapter is all about preparing you to choose a direction and level of implementation for your plan. There are so many variables for you to consider, many of which I am not aware of while writing this book. For instance, your ability to comprehend and retain the information; the tools, such as a spare computer, that you have available; your budget; your living circumstances; and your ability to have access to the target computer or cell phone to accomplish what you need to do.

Remember that you don't need a big budget. In fact, if you are resourceful and already have administrative access to the computer, you can do this for absolutely no money at all. Most of your costs could be avoided by borrowing a USB drive from a friend. Most, if not all, of the software utilities that I cover in my book allow you to use them for a short time period without purchase.

Even if you don't have administrative access to the computer, the application that will change your security level can be purchased for only $49.00. You can also purchase used and new USB drives for a much lower cost on places like eBay. It is up to you just how much you will be able to accomplish and it will depend mostly on your level of determination. I said that in the beginning and I mean it now.

This chapter cannot provide specifics to every situation that may arise, so the information in this chapter will be flexible. You can then modify what you need to in order to adapt and make a sensible plan that meets your circumstances and goals. Remember, it is not always about imaging the hard drive; you can start by taking small steps.

Taking small steps may be accomplished by connecting your spouse's computer to an external USB drive and then **Copying** their PROFILE folder, as well as other folders, that store their email to that USB drive. This will provide you with a lot of information you need to review without the need to perform computer forensics. There is no doubt you will be missing some information, but you can always image the drive later if you feel you need additional information. If you take this route please remember how to avoid the "copying error" that is caused as you attempt to copy the PROFILE folder when you are logged in as that user. Windows will not allow you to copy files that are in use and I covered this issue in Chapter 5.

Small steps may also include becoming familiar with your spouse's cell phone and then manually reviewing the cell phone, as well as the cell phone records. It's not always about purchasing products or services, but it is always about getting organized and staying focused if you want to be successful. So let's go through a plan of action that is broken down into several steps and will give you what you need to accomplish in order to be successful.

I have designed this plan so you may start with small steps or just jump to the part that gives you the ability to dive in headfirst and start imaging hard drives. The flexibility is built into the plan and the option where to start and end is up to you. However, I am not there with you, so you are the eyes and ears of the implementation. You have to know what you need to accomplish in order to schedule it on the plan.

Documenting Your Findings

I have been an investigator for most of my adult life. I have learned from experience that most cases were successful because of the steps people took before they started a case, as opposed to information they tried to recall later. It is important for you to document your findings as you identify crucial information or you may forget about the information altogether.

The best way to start is to get a notebook that has several partitions or purchase one that enables you to partition it yourself. It is up to you to decide how you want to organize your findings, and it is important to work the way that makes you comfortable.

One section of your notebook may document the findings you obtained from your spouse's cell phone, another may document the findings from your spouse's computer, and yet another partition may document the findings you obtained from your spouse's e-mail accounts. The important objective for documenting your findings is to be able to link bits of crucial information to other information, so the notebook must be logical, based on your train of thought – not how I might organize information, but how you would. In addition, it helps you to organize the information you need to later confront your spouse. These findings may be in the form of computer printouts, hard copies of bills, and personal notes you made identifying links between disparate information.

182 • Cyber Lies

It is important to make sure that you print information or documents as you identify them if they contain important information. If you tell yourself that you will print them later, then you may forget about it all together. Remember you are analyzing a computer that can potentially have literally thousands of text documents and graphic files. Don't wait, print them out and place them in the appropriate notebook partition immediately.

Developing the Initial Plan

This plan assumes that you want to start slowly and work your way into the process by getting an overview of what your spouse may be up to. Remember this section is designed to help you organize your efforts; it will not review what was covered in the previous chapters so it is important to have read everything up to this point. The best place to start will be to review their Web cache, browser history, documents, pictures, and e-mail.

The Web cache and browser history will give you an idea of what websites your spouse visits, if they have online Web-based e-mail accounts, and if they are involved in certain Web forums – including the dating and cheating sites. Hopefully, you read the prior chapters and started to become familiar with these types of sites and technologies. It is the only way you are going to know what you are looking for. If you have not done so yet, then I suggest you collect the data you need and then review these types of sites before you begin to analyze your spouse's computer. Remember, though: *Never use your spouse's computer to visit these sites, or you will be placing the information on their computer yourself.* Also: *Never use your own personal computer or your spouse may believe you're up to no good if they are looking at your computer.* There is a lot to remember and to be cautious about.

Where are you going to get all that information? What are you going to need to accomplish this? These are not rhetorical questions, so please take a minute and think about them. Then continue to read to see if you are correct. I want you to start to think about the information because it will help you start to develop the expert in you.

Copy Profile Folder to External USB Drive

The information that you are looking to obtain such as Web cache, documents, pictures, and e-mail – are all located in a PROFILE folder for your spouse. The PROFILE folder is the same name as the USERNAME they use to login to the computer. So, if their USERNAME was JSMITH, the PROFILE folder would be JSMITH. If all you see is an ADMINIS-TRATOR folder, then they are logging in as ADMINISTRATOR. The profiles for the computer are located in the DOCUMENTS AND SETTINGS folder. So, all you need to do is copy your spouse's PROFILE folder located in the DOCUMENTS AND SETTINGS folder to an external USB drive. It is important to know your spouse's login name, as you want to make sure you are looking at their information and not one of the other profiles that your spouse does not use. These other PROFILE folders may belong to children, if you have any.

The only device you will need at this time is an external USB drive. So make sure you do your research and purchase one that is going to suit your needs, which means make sure it has enough storage capacity not only to copy what you need now, but also if you want to image your spouse's hard drive in the future.

This section assumes that you know how to copy specific PROFILE folders located in the DOCUMENTS AND SETTINGS folder to your external USB drive and will not cover that process. However, refer to Chapter 5 that discusses the Windows file system if you need to know how or go to our website for additional information.

Get Administrative Access

Is there anything else you might need? Did you ask yourself this question: *Do I have administrative access to the computer I want to analyze?* That is an important question and will determine if you can even analyze the computer. You may have to purchase a product that will allow you to bypass system security so you can change your security level.

Have Appropriate Application Software or File Viewer

You are also going to need an application installed for every file type you want to view, or you will have to purchase some type of file viewer that will enable you to view multiple types of file formats. While there are many products that you can locate and purchase by performing keyword searches using **File viewer** as the keyword in your favorite search engine, for the purposes of this exercise, I am using Explorer View. This gives you the look and feel of using Microsoft Windows Explorer and you can instantly view several file types including graphics files, Word documents, PDF files, Excel files, and many more.

Have an Appropriate E-mail Viewer

Since you also want to view e-mail, you will need the appropriate e-mail viewer. DBXanalyzer is one of the easy ones to learn to use for .DBX files, which Microsoft Outlook Express uses to store e-mail messages. So you have to know which e-mail client your spouse uses prior to analyzing this type of data. If you are unsure, please refer to the chapter that discusses locating, retrieving, and analyzing e-mail. You have to make sure that all of the viewing applications are installed on the computer that you will be using to analyze the PROFILE folders prior to starting the analysis. Remember, that not all e-mail is stored in the PROFILE folders, which is why you need to know the location of the e-mail files for each application. In addition, different versions store their files in different locations as well.

When you have the PROFILE folders on your external USB drive, you need to bring that to a computer where you can look through it. The best place to accomplish this is at a friend's house or when your spouse is not at home and you use a separate computer to analyze that folder and all of the data.

Reviewing Your Research

Graphic Files

1) Turn the **Computer ON** and connect the external USB drive to that computer.

2) **Start** Explorer View application.

3) **Navigate** your way to the folder that holds the Web cache for your spouse. You should be able to view all of the graphics in this window. **Double-clicking on any one of the images brings that picture up in a larger format.** Take your time to review all of the images to make the best assessment. On the bottom of the screen, you can see how to do a variety of activities, which include **Saving** the file to another folder or even **Printing** it. You may opt to **Print** the picture and then **Save** the picture in a separate folder titled CRUCIAL PICTURES. This way you can locate the important ones quickly without have to look through all of the pictures again.

E-mail Files

1) Using Explorer View, navigate your way to the e-mail folder that contains your spouse's e-mail.

2) If you are looking to view .DBX files, then just highlight the appropriate .DBX file and Explorer View will turn over the file to the appropriate e-mail viewer.

3) If you use Explorer View and **Double-click** on the INBOX.DBX. This will start the DBXanalyzer application and the INBOX.DBX will automatically open that file and allow you to view it using DBXanalyzer.

Other Files

1) Navigate your way through the MYDOCUMENTS, MYPIC-TURES, TEMPORARY INTERNET, BROWSER HISTORY, and FAVORITES folders, as well as every other folder in the appro-priate profiles. Make sure you understand which PROFILE

folder you are in and that you know your spouse uses that profile when they login before you accuse them of doing something that they really did not do. If you are unsure, then please review the chapter that discusses the Windows file system (or check with a friend who has a technical background if you are still unsure).

Cell Phone Files

Now let's address your spouse's cell phone. It may appear that this will be a lot quicker, but you need to do your research if you want your cell phone analyzing activities to be as fruitful as your computer forensic activities. There is a lot to understand in order to know where to look, and a lot of things to remember to check if you want to find out as much as you can.

The first step is to find out as much as you can regarding your spouse's cell phone. If you know very little about cell phone technology, or your spouse has a cell phone that is a newer phone which has many neat features, then I would consider a trip to the local phone store for a lesson or two on the phone itself. You should make note of all the features your spouse's cell phone had so you don't miss any as you start to analyze the cell phone.

Once you are comfortable in gaining access to the phone, I would start to look at every available feature that they were using. Cell phone logs, e-mail, pictures, Web history, quick messages, and especially text-messages. Since this is a manual exercise and you are not performing cell phone forensics, you need to make sure you have the time and materials to take good notes.

Once you are taking notes – whether it is a note for a call log, e-mail, or text-message – make sure that you not only record the message itself but also the originating number or e-mail address it was from, the date, the time, the duration, and as much information as you can. You have the phone in front of you and I don't, so only you will know what you may be missing. Don't miss anything! Take your time and never take the shortcut because you believe it will make things go faster. If you keep this in mind, you will be successful.

Developing an Advanced Plan

Never analyze a computer or cell phone image file while your spouse is in the house.

Imaging the Hard Drive

This section is for individuals who have decided to take their efforts to an advanced stage. Remember, this section is designed to help you organize your efforts; it will not review what was covered in the previous chapters, so it is important to have read everything up to this point. This plan includes the imaging of the computer hard drive and cell phone to ensure that you have what you need.

While it may be easier to start off slowly, especially when you are new to the process, there are times when you need to act quickly to get copies of everything (for example, your spouse is moving out and they are taking the computer with them). TJhis is when time is of the essence so you need to plan, focus, and perform immediately.

We are going to start off with the computer. Ask yourself: *What will I need to do to accomplish a full image and analysis of the hard drive?* Let's start with the following questions:

Do I have administrative access to the computer? If not, then you need to purchase a product that will enable you to bypass the security of the computer so you can gain administrative access to that computer. It would be great to practice on a friend's computer so you know what to expect when you use it on your spouse's computer.

Do I have access to a friend's desktop computer or laptop computer? If not, then you may need to purchase a used computer to perform certain tasks, especially during the analysis phase of your efforts. This is going to be a crucial piece of equipment during the setup and analysis phase.

What other hardware do I need? How about the external USB drive? This is the one device that you will use during all phases of your computer forensic activities – the imaging process to store the forensic images of your spouse's computer; storing all of the forensic utilities;

and applications that you will need to perform the analysis of your spouse's computer.

Between reading the chapter on analyzing computers and this chapter, you should have a very good idea of how to proceed. The best way to make sure that you have everything is to image a friend's hard drive. If you don't have a friend's hard drive, then you can image the laptop computer you are using. Remember, practice makes perfect. The more you have practiced, the more prepared you will be; and the more prepared you are, the more successful you will be.

Our corporate policy states that if a forensic technician is going out in the field to image a hard drive, they must first image a hard drive in our office with the same equipment that they are taking with them. Once that has been completed, they must open that image to ensure they were successful. This is the only way to ensure success.

Imaging the Cell Phone

Now it's time to image your spouse's cell phone. The best time to image the cell phone is when your spouse is sleeping. Depending on the cell phone and the power of the computer you are using, it may take anywhere from ten to twenty minutes to image the cell phone.

Once you image the cell phone, remember not to be tempted to start the analysis. Place the cell phone back and resume your normal schedule; if you had been sleeping, it's time to get back to bed. It is easy to get caught during your forensic activity and there is no need to jeopardize your efforts. Get the image and get back to bed.

Long before you are ready to image your spouse's cell phone you need to prepare in order to be successful.

1) Getting all the information about your spouse's cell phone is the first place to start.

2) In order to image the cell phone, you will need to purchase forensic software. Depending on what phone your spouse has, it may be necessary to purchase PDA seizure software and not cell seizure software, which is the case with Palm® Treo™.

PalmTreo use the Palm operating system and therefore requires the PDA seizure software, despite the fact that it is a cell phone. As technology evolves, it can throw us a curve ball but we can still hit it out of the park if we ask the right questions as we plan. Be diligent.

3) When you are on the phone with the company you are purchasing the forensic software from, you need to ask the right questions to make sure you are not only getting the right product, but also getting a cable that will connect your spouse's cell phone to the computer you are using as a forensic computer.

4) You also want to make sure you are getting a product that does not have to be registered online, so it works as soon as you install it. This is sometimes accomplished with an embedded key, so ask about that when you are on the phone with the company. If you don't, you may have to get over another hurdle by getting your laptop computer online if it is not already.

5) Now that you are sure you have everything you need, it is time to set up a date and time to accomplish the acquisition. Let's say that it is going to be late Friday night, around 3 a.m. Saturday morning. The end of a week can often take a toll on most of us and we are usually looking to sleep late on Saturday morning. Saturday night into Sunday morning is also a good time.

6) Set up your forensic acquisition unit far from where your spouse sleeps, perhaps in the basement of your home. Make sure to turn **OFF** the computer speaker when booting it up in the middle of the night.

7) Leave the cell phone where it always is until you are ready. That cell phone should always remain where your spouse places it except for the twenty minutes or so it takes to image the phone.

8) As soon as the image is complete, get the cell phone back where you found it and then dismantle your cell phone acquisition setup and turn it **OFF** for the night. Go to bed and analyze it during the week when you have the time alone.

Afterword

I have attempted to cover as much information as possible in order to increase your potential for success. I want you to succeed and I want you to gain access to exactly what you need to see, not only to protect yourself and make decisions, but also to answer that age-old question: *Am I crazy?*

As technology evolves, devices not only change, but new technologies are created. Feel free to use the CyberLies.com website as your main resource – not only to address your questions, but also to continue to keep up with the changes in this industry.

I would also like to receive your feedback regarding *Cyber Lies* and your success with locating, retrieving, reviewing, and analyzing information stored on technological devices. Remember, you're not a spy; you're entitled.

I wish you well.

John Paul Lucich
April 2006

Glossary

Acquire–The process of imaging a hard drive for the subsequent analysis. (See Forensic Image)

BIOS–An acronym that means Basic Input/Output System. A chipset located inside your computer that stores instructions for the computer.

.BMP–A file extension used to identify a specific file format that stores a still (not-moving) graphic picture.

Boot Sequence–The sequence that the computer uses while attempting to load the operating system. The default boot sequence in most computers is set to look for the operating system first using the CD-ROM and then the computer's hard drive.

Byte–A byte is contained of eight bits but is more commonly referred to as a character or a space. (The word BYTE contains four bytes.)

CMOS–An acronym that means Complementary Metal Oxide Semiconductor. The configuration of the computer is stored in the CMOS, which can be accessed and modified.

Computer Forensics–A methodology and process used to acquire storage media and to authenticate, preserve, and retrieve data.

Data Recovery–A methodology and process used to recover data that has been lost due to a physical or logical hard drive problem.

.DBX–A file extension used to identify a Microsoft Outlook Express mail file.

.DOC–A file extension used to identify a Microsoft Word document.

Documents and Settings—A folder located in the root of the drive that stores all user profiles, as well as all user data. This folder stores the most valuable information that spouse's seek to analyze. (See Root.)

.E01 file—A file extension used to identify an industry file format used by forensic technicians to acquire and store an exact copy of a hard drive.

File—A computer file stored in a specific format that is accessed by a software program in order to view or edit the file.

File Extension—The last three or four characters that follow the filename (and separated from the filename by a dot {.}). For example: In the file, mypicturefile.gif, gif is the file extension.

File System—A system of storing files on a hard drive. A few examples include: FAT16, FAT32, and NTFS.

Folder—A file structure that allows users to store files by category or type.

Forensic Image—An exact copy of a hard drive, including the files system, as well as the deleted and unallocated areas of the hard drive.

.GIF—A file extension used to identify a specific file format that stores a still graphic picture.

Gigabyte—The measurement of 1 billion bytes of data, or 1024 megabytes. Today, a typical hard drive stores between 40 to 80 gigabytes of data. A byte is one character or space.

Hard Drive—A device inside a computer that stores data.

Instant-messaging—Also known as IM. A software product that enables two or more people to have a text-based chat over the Internet in real-time.

JPG—Also known as JPEG. A file extension used to identify a specific file format that stores a still (not moving) graphic picture.

Keylogger—A hardware device or software program used to capture the keystrokes of a user for later analysis.

Kilobyte–The measurement of 1000 bytes or, specifically in binary systems, 1024 bytes. A byte is one character or space.

Megabyte–The measurement of 1,000,000 bytes of data, or 1024 Kilobytes. A byte is one character or space.

MOV–A file extension used to identify a QuickTime file format that stores a video file.

.MPG–Also known as .mpeg. A file extension used to identify a specific file format that stores a video file.

Operating System–Software that controls the flow of information among the devices of a computer. Examples include: Windows XP, Windows2000, MAC OS 10, and Linux.

Peripheral–A device that is attached to a computer. Examples include: a mouse, printer, and keyboard, to name a few.

PDA–An acronym that means Personal Digital Assistant. A hardware device that is similar to a pocket computer. Used to create and store data, as well as communicate via e-mail.

PFC–An acronym that means Personal Filing Cabinet. This is the file that stores the AOL e-mail and file attachments. It has no file extension. In order to view the file, the file must be renamed using the file extension .pfc.

Protocol–A set of rules that define how to accomplish a specific task. Protocols are used to define how to send and receive e-mail and much more.

.PST–A file extension used to identify a Microsoft Outlook mail file.

Root–The entry to the hard drive file structure that is not located in any folder. The base hierarchy of the computer's file system.

Search engine–A searchable online database of Internet resources. One popular search engine is Google.

Snoopware—Also known as spyware. An application that records the activity of a user and saves the data for later analysis. These applications can also provide user activity reports in real-time.

.SXW—A file extension used to identify a StarOffice text document. StarOffice is a trademark of the Sun Microsystems.

Sync Software—A software application used to synchronize data between a cell phone and computer, or a PDA (Personal Digital Assistant) and a computer. This should not be used to capture and analyze data or it could result in the destruction of data.

.TIF—Also known as .TIFF. A file extension used to identify a specific file format that stores a still (not-moving) graphic picture.

USB Drive—An external hard drive that connects to the computer via the USB port. USB hard drives are available in a variety of sizes and capacities.

Web Portal—A website that offers a variety of services and provides access to an array of resources and content.

Windows—A trademark of the Microsoft Corporation used to identify an operating system or file system.

.WMV—A file extension used to identify a specific file format that stores a video file.

Index

Computer Forensic Boot Camp for Spouses

One day hands-on training for those interested in learning how to image, recover and analyze the data found on computers.

**Call (888) 674-4872
or send an email to
info@cyberlies.com
for additional information.**

DISCARD